THE GREAT
HISPANIC HERITAGE

Antonio López
de Santa Anna

THE GREAT HISPANIC HERITAGE

Isabel Allende

Simón Bolívar

Jorge Luis Borges

Miguel de Cervantes

Cesar Chavez

Roberto Clemente

Celia Cruz

Salvador Dalí

Oscar De La Hoya

Oscar de la Renta

America Ferrera

Francisco Goya

Ernesto "Che" Guevara

Dolores Huerta

Frida Kahlo, Second
   Edition

Jennifer Lopez

Gabriel García Márquez

José Martí

Pedro Martinez

Ellen Ochoa

Eva Perón

Pablo Picasso

Juan Ponce de León

Tito Puente

Manny Ramirez

Diego Rivera, Second
   Edition

Antonio López de Santa
   Anna

Carlos Santana

Sammy Sosa

Pancho Villa

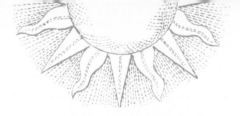

THE GREAT
HISPANIC HERITAGE

Antonio López de Santa Anna

Brenda Lange

CHELSEA HOUSE
PUBLISHERS
An imprint of Infobase Publishing

Chelsea House
An imprint of Infobase Publishing
132 West 31st Street
New York NY 10001

Library of Congress Cataloging-in-Publication Data
Lange, Brenda.
  Antonio López de Santa Anna / Brenda Lange.
    p. cm. — (Great Hispanic heritage)
  Includes bibliographical references and index.
  ISBN 978-1-60413-734-7 (hardcover : alk. paper) 1. Santa Anna, Antonio López de, 1794?-1876—Juvenile literature. 2. Presidents—Mexico—Biography—Juvenile literature. 3. Generals—Mexico—Biography—Juvenile literature. 4. Mexico—History—1821-1861—Juvenile literature. 5. Texas—History—To 1846—Juvenile literature. 6. Alamo (San Antonio, Tex.)—Siege, 1836—Juvenile literature. I. Title. II. Series.
  F1232.S232L37 2010
  972'.04092—dc22
  [B]   2010007515

Chelsea House books are available at special discounts when purchased in bulk quantities for businesses, associations, institutions, or sales promotions. Please call our Special Sales Department in New York at (212) 967-8800 or (800) 322-8755.

You can find Chelsea House on the World Wide Web at http://www.chelseahouse.com

Text design by Terry Mallon
Cover design by Terry Mallon/Alicia Post
Composition by EJB Publishing Services
Cover printed by Bang Printing, Brainerd, MN
Book printed and bound by Bang Printing, Brainerd, MN
Date printed: August 2010
Printed in the United States of America

10 9 8 7 6 5 4 3 2 1

This book is printed on acid-free paper.

All links and Web addresses were checked and verified to be correct at the time of publication. Because of the dynamic nature of the Web, some addresses and links may have changed since publication and may no longer be valid.

Contents

1   Remember the Alamo   6

2   Santa Anna's Early Life   9

3   The Land Santa Anna Loved   18

4   Santa Anna's Early Career   28

5   A New Republic   39

6   The Road to the Alamo   51

7   The Alamo and San Jacinto   63

8   Santa Anna's Later Years   71

Chronology and Timeline   89

Notes   93

Bibliography   94

Further Reading   95

Index   97

Remember
the Alamo

All was darkness inside the walls of the Alamo, where nearly
two dozen women and children slept, protected within the
walls of the mission church. It was cramped, hot, and airless
inside the tiny rooms. They had taken refuge there nearly two
weeks earlier when the Mexican army first marched into the
village of San Antonio de Bexar. Outside the church itself,
but within the compound walls, their husbands, fathers, and
brothers camped and kept watch against the encroaching
enemy army.

Shortly before daybreak on March 6, 1836, the quiet of
the chilly morning was broken by the sudden sounding of a
Mexican bugle, followed by the tramping of thousands of feet,
the calling out of Spanish commands, and then the crack of
gunshots and booming of cannons. The attack on the Alamo
had begun. As nearly 1,800 of his men, on foot and horseback,
surrounded and attacked the Alamo's walls, commanding

During the last stand at the Alamo, fewer than 200 Texas rebels fought valiantly but were vastly outnumbered by the Mexican army. The fate of these defenders, along with their wives and children, lay in the hands of Mexican general Antonio López de Santa Anna.

officer General Antonio López de Santa Anna sat hundreds of yards away, watching. He appeared like royalty on his tall stallion. Dressed characteristically in his grand uniform, his black eyes blazed under a carefully combed shock of black hair. His officers knew what they were doing, yet he was anxious, tensed for the battle, with a need to control every move and action.

The sky quickly turned pink and blue, and soldiers from both sides were silhouetted on top of the dark stone walls, obscured by smoke and flames that shot up each time a cannonball hit its mark. Hundreds of Mexican soldiers climbed up and over the walls; as those in the front lines would fall, others quickly scrambled over them and into the compound. Fewer than 200 Alamo defenders fought valiantly but were no match, outnumbered as they were by more than nine to one. The fighting quickly turned to hand-to-hand combat. Too close to fire their long rifles, David Crockett's Tennessee regulars swung their guns like clubs, knocking down the Mexicans in their path, then using their sharp bayonets to finish them off. The Mexicans also had bayonets attached to their guns, and many defenders died the same way.

The women and children huddled together in the church sacristy, hiding under bales of hay or wooden crates, just trying to stay alive. The smell of burning buildings and animals, along with the screams and groans of wounded and dying men, must have been nearly overwhelming. But it was all over almost before it began. By 7:00 that morning, every male defender had been killed or captured. The women and children were brought to meet the Mexican commander, Santa Anna. As this was happening, he gave the order to execute the handful of male prisoners.

Santa Anna's Early Life

Antonio de Padua María Severino López de Santa Anna y Pérez de Lebrón was born on February 21, 1794, in the city of Xalapa (sometimes spelled Jalapa and pronounced "ha-lapa") in the Mexican state of Veracruz.

Santa Anna was one of seven children in a middle-class family that lived in a large house in the center of the town—in the *centro histórico*. They moved several times when he was a boy—to the port city of Veracruz and back again. In many ways a typical middle-class family, they were financially comfortable, although not rich. They owned a little property, and the children received an education. Santa Anna loved the area and spent much of his life in that region—living on two haciendas (estates), Manga de Clavo and El Encero, or in an apartment in Mexico City—when he was not out battling Indians, Texians, or otherwise fighting for Mexican independence.

This 1834 engraving by Carlos Nebel shows the town square of Veracruz, Mexico, Santa Anna's home base. Veracruz was the principle port city for Mexico and Spain.

When Santa Anna was three, his family moved to Teziutlán, a border city between Veracruz and Puebla, northwest of Xalapa. The family returned in two years but then moved to Veracruz in 1800. When he was 13, he again moved back to Xalapa with his siblings and his mother, Manuela Pérez Lebrón, and father, Antonio López Santa Anna, but again stayed only about two years and returned to the port city. He considered himself a Xalapeño (someone from Xalapa); however, he spent so much time in the port city that he became more of a *porteño* (someone born in the port city). He ultimately was comfortable and at home in both places. Santa Anna was closest to his sister, Francisca, and his brother, Manuel. Manuel followed him into the army in 1812, fought in the War of Independence, and later followed him into the political world of Xalapa. Francisca conspired in 1832 to bring Santa Anna back to power, and she was imprisoned for her loyalty to her brother.

By 1824, Santa Anna owned the largest home in Xalapa and depended on his connections with politicians, financiers, merchants, and other influential people to bankroll his military campaigns and to back him politically. Three bankers from this city handled his finances throughout his life, and other businessmen provided financial support for two of his revolts: on September 12, 1828, and September 9, 1841. His support helped the city develop a textile industry in the 1830s and 1840s, and he served as its vice governor, governor, and military commander over the years. During the height of his popularity, when he returned home from the capital city or from military campaigns, bands would play and the city would celebrate his visit with fiestas. It is not surprising that he always liked Xalapa and maintained ties to it.

XALAPA

The first European to set foot in the region was Spanish conquistador Hernán Cortés. In 1519, he found a thriving Aztec Indian settlement along the coast. Four native cultures originally had settled in this area, eventually joining to form one large village in the early 1300s. Overcome by the Aztecs at the end of the 1400s, the area was considered Aztec territory until Cortés landed. After Spain conquered the Aztecs, the Spanish claimed the area, settled it, and turned the port into a destination for ships from the homeland. The inland city of Xalapa became famous for an annual fair at which goods from Spain were bought and sold. It was an important hub for the trading of goods from the coast to inland areas, including Mexico City. By the time Santa Anna was born, the city was struggling with a recession. However, Viceroy José de Iturrigaray helped with its resurgence by providing financial backing for the business class. Until around 1860, Xalapa was the busiest city in Veracruz and the state's main financial center. After that time, the railroad was built from Mexico City to the city of Veracruz by way of the mountain town of Orizaba, bypassing Xalapa and robbing it of some of its importance.

Today, Xalapa is known for the processing of locally grown coffee, tobacco, and fruit—bananas, mangoes, avocados, limes, and chilies. Other local industry includes the manufacture of cigarettes and processed food and beverages. Residents are also employed in the government sector and in education, including at Veracruz University. Xalapa is the capital of the state of Veracruz, which is about 600 miles (965.6 kilometers) long, located almost midway on the coast of the Gulf of Mexico. Xalapa has about 400,000 inhabitants and is located about 60 miles (96.56 km) northwest of the port city of Veracruz, which is about 200 miles (321.87 km) east of Mexico City. At about 4,600 feet (1,402 meters) above sea level, Xalapa is part of a tropical forest, and it is generally foggy and very humid. Lush and verdant, it is often known as the City of Flowers. To the west, the mountain Cofre de Perote looms over the city, with the volcano Pico de Orizaba (the highest mountain in the country at 18,490 feet, or 5,635.75 m) towering over them all.

Frances Erskine Calderón de la Barca was born in Scotland and married the Spanish minister to Mexico. She lived in that country for two years during his public service and kept a diary that was later published as a book, *Life in Mexico,* in 1843. Her description of Xalapa:

> It consists of little more than a few steep streets, very old, with some large and excellent houses, the best as usual belonging to English merchants, and many to those of Veracruz, who come to live in or near Jalapa, during the reign of the "vomito" [the common name for yellow fever]. There are some old churches, a very old convent of Franciscan monks, and a well-supplied marketplace. Everywhere there are flowers—roses creeping over the old walls, Indian girls making green garlands for the virgin and saints, flowers in the shops, flowers at the windows,

Hernán Cortés is depicted at a banquet for envoys of Montezuma. Cortés was the first Spaniard to set foot in the region, and he swiftly conquered the area's inhabitants, the Aztecs.

but, above all, everywhere one of the most splendid mountain views in the world.

About Veracruz, de la Barca wrote that she was bothered by the mosquitoes and humidity, and that the city was ugly and sad. She called it "miserable, melancholy, forlorn, and black-looking,"[1] and she could not understand how outsiders became attached to the city. She was, however, impressed with the pride that native Veracruzanos had for it.

THE PORT CITY OF VERACRUZ

Around the turn of the nineteenth century, about 16,000 people lived in Veracruz, making it bigger than Xalapa. But during the Mexican War of Independence, the population dropped to almost 7,000. The port city was busy, dirty, and noisy compared to Xalapa, especially when fleets of merchant ships arrived. Inhabitants included Indians and mestizos (mixed Spanish Americans/Spanish Indians) who came to Veracruz for work, to watch the foreigners, and to sell crafts. The population ebbed and flowed with the fleets, with those from outlying areas coming into town to buy and sell merchandise and leaving when the ships sailed.

Few whites lived there, because of their fear of yellow fever, a scourge throughout most of the nineteenth century. Foreign travelers feared the city because of this disease, and rightfully so. Symptoms of the virus included worsening fever and headaches, fatigue, and, in later stages, black vomit and bleeding from the nose and gums. Many of the 40,000 troops sent by Spain between 1811 and 1818 died from yellow fever. Anyone born and raised in the region was immune to yellow fever, including Santa Anna, but it was deadly to those without this natural immunity. (The disease was eradicated early in the twentieth century.) Santa Anna's immunity gave him an advantage against enemies from outside the region and acted as a defense for the city. He could outlast a siege, knowing his army of local soldiers could too, while the attackers had to get in and out as quickly as possible. Many Afro-Caribbean people (descended from those originally brought as slaves to work the sugarcane and cotton plantations) occupied the city in spite of the threat of disease. One of the oldest cities in the country, Veracruz endured raiding by pirates, a French occupation, and a brief American occupation. Today, the city is a tourist destination.

Almost all the trade between Spain and Mexico—known at the time as New Spain—came through the important port of Veracruz. Imports included wine, oil, mercury, iron, clothes, paper, and books. Silver, leather, indigo, wool, wood, sugar, tobacco, vanilla, and coffee were among the exports. The city's architecture was a jumble of wooden huts and walled-in store-houses. The overall atmosphere was unhealthy. Anyone who had money, and was able, lived at a higher altitude, away from the chaotic city and the threat of disease.

FINDING HIS CALLING

Because his base was here, Santa Anna had access to supplies at the wharf and to the financial backing of merchants. This support helped him in his military campaigns, and the two

WAGING A WAR OF WORDS

Sometimes, outrageous offers were made to entice Americans to immigrate to Texas and join the cause for independence. Broadsides (posters) offering 800 acres (323.75 hectares) of land to anyone willing to settle in Texas and join the fight for independence from Mexico were put up across the South just before the siege of San Antonio. They called Texas "the Garden of America" and offered free passage to the territory in addition to the land.

Other broadsides were used to wage negative public relations campaigns against the Mexicans, especially its leaders. One such broadside called Santa Anna "the usurper of the South." It implied that he wanted to make slaves out of Texans and that his troops would brutally attack the territory's women.

roads leading to Mexico City provided him a strategic advantage. Because he was raised in both Veracruz and Xalapa, he knew many people in power and was loyal to both cities. His entire family—on both sides—came from Veracruz, and this history gave him unique access. His family was solidly middle-class creole, of the criollo class, meaning they were born in a Spanish colony but were of "pure" Spanish ancestry. Some say he was part mestizo, or of mixed lineage—part Spanish and part Indian—but this has not been proved. However, if the common people *thought* he was criollo, that may help explain his popularity. Although the family was not rich, they were connected to the merchant class, the upper class, and even the workers, thanks to his father's participation in the city's politics. Santa Anna's father, Antonio López, graduated from university and was a lawyer, mortgage broker, and businessman and held several minor municipal positions.

Santa Anna's mother was known as a religious woman. She was outspoken and extremely loyal; she protected her friends when necessary. This trait once landed her in court for questioning by the Inquisition, for defending friends who had a party and played music that was not approved by the Catholic Church. Santa Anna's father had insisted he become a shopkeeper and even withdrew his son from school to set him up as an apprentice to the merchant José Cos. Santa Anna did not last long in that position, and he told his father he was not born to be a ragman. He found his true calling at 16, when, with his mother's blessing, he lied about his age and joined the Spanish army on July 6, 1810. Sixty-four years later, Santa Anna wrote: "From my first years, I was inclined toward the glorious career at arms and felt a true vocation for army life. I gained my parents' consent and became a gentleman cadet in the Fixed Infantry Regiment of Veracruz."[2]

His parents were royalists, or those who supported Spain's rule, and they hoped to continue to be successful under Spain's authority. However, they also were part of the class that turned to the cause of independence once war began. Santa Anna's solid, middle-class upbringing had made him initially popular among the other soldiers, and his heroism in battle earned him individual respect. His ability to fit in with all classes helped him immeasurably once independence was attained. He was comfortable mingling with the lower classes, gambling and socializing with them. His military career allowed him special privileges and social ranking and access. Class structure ultimately did not matter or make a difference to Santa Anna.

3

The Land Santa Anna Loved

Santa Anna participated in many battles in the northern reaches of his country and across the border into the territory known as Texas. He loved the long vistas and the roughness of the plains. He was comfortable among the wildlife and in the extremes of weather. He felt such an affinity for the area that he felt at home when he led thousands of soldiers against the defenders at the Alamo and in the battles that followed. It is helpful to understand the region as it was when European explorers first set foot in this land, and before.

Hundreds of years before white settlers made their way to the area known today as Texas, many different Indian tribes called it home. Some of these Indians were the Apache, Comanche, Caddo, Tonkawa, and Karankawa. The Coahuiltecans, made up of almost 200 tribes with similar cultures, also inhabited the area. Each tribe had distinctive characteristics, as did the land it inhabited. Some tribes lived on the dry, desolate, flat, grassy plains; others lived along the coastline, where swamps, marshes, and barrier islands were common.

The Apache were a powerful people, considered fierce warriors by the American army. They were often at war with the Spanish and Americans. The Comanche were hunter-gatherers of the plains in what is now the American Southwest. They were the first Indians to make horses a part of their every-day life, and they introduced them to other Plains Indians. Originally from East Texas and western Louisiana, the Caddo were nearly destroyed by smallpox brought in by Spanish and French missionaries. The Tonkawa were nomadic, traveling in search of game. They used bows and arrows until the Spanish introduced them to guns. The Karankawa lived along the Gulf Coast of what is now Texas and died off as a result of illness and wars with the white settlers.

THE ARRIVAL OF MEN WITH WHITE SKIN

The Caribbean islands of Santo Domingo, Puerto Rico, and Jamaica were the first lands in the New World to come under Spanish control. After that, Ponce de León came to Florida in 1513, officially beginning Spanish exploration in North America. Spain initially sent the conquistadors to North America in search of gold and silver, instructing them to claim the riches of the Indians. At the same time, they were expected to "save" the Indians' souls by converting them to Roman Catholicism.

Alonso Álvarez de Pineda landed in Texas in 1519; he was the first Spaniard to arrive there. The Spanish also made land-fall in Mexico that year. Hernán Cortés led the first landing party and founded the first settlement in Mexico. He landed on Good Friday, known as La Vera Cruz ("The True Cross"), and named the settlement La Villa Rica de la Vera Cruz. Veracruz became the principal port for Mexico—known then as New Spain—and main point of communication between Spain and New Spain, and it would become Santa Anna's home base about 250 years later. Several years after the Cortés

POLITICAL HISTORY OF MEXICO

The area we know today as Mexico is bordered to the north by the United States and to the south by Guatemala and Belize. It also is bordered by the Pacific Ocean, Gulf of Mexico, and Caribbean Sea. Before the first Spanish conquistadors, or conquerors, arrived in 1519, led by Hernán Cortés, this land was home to several great Indian tribes, including the Aztec. For 300 years after Spanish soldiers, settlers, and missionaries landed and settled the region, it was a colony of Spain known as New Spain.

In 1810, the Mexican people revolted and, following an 11-year struggle, declared their country an independent republic. The country had some trouble settling into its new identity, however, and this time was characterized by economic instability and revolts. During the next 50 years, Mexico was ruled by several dictators, two emperors, and many presidents.

Originally, Mexico included the areas that are now the American states of Texas, California, Nevada, and Utah, as well as parts of Arizona, New Mexico, Wyoming, and Colorado. The region of Texas was first lost in 1836 when settlers there declared their freedom. Texas was recognized as an independent republic by the United States as well as most of the rest of the world.

Mexico, however, never wanted to acknowledge this loss of territory and went to war with the United States (1846–1848) partly over its claim to Texas. After U.S. troops took Mexico City, the Mexican government agreed to the Treaty of Guadalupe Hidalgo, which is how Mexico lost almost half its territory, including the land encompassing the previously mentioned states.

Since 1920, Mexico has experienced a series of social and economic reforms, and today it exists as a federal constitutional republic, governed by three branches of government and holds open and free elections. Mexico has three political parties, and its capital is Mexico City.

expedition, Pánfilo de Narváez, an explorer who had been to Mexico once before, was given permission to settle "Florida," which then applied to the vast, semicircular expanse of land from the Gulf Coast of Florida to the Gulf Coast of Mexico. In 1523, Cortés defeated the Indians living along the coast north of Veracruz and founded Santiesteban del Puerto on the banks of the Pánuco River. All this exploration began based on rumors that cities of gold had been discovered by earlier explorers.

In 1528, Álvar Núñez Cabeza de Vaca landed on the Gulf Coast of what is now Texas with about two dozen other Spanish explorers. They had been part of the large group led by Narváez. The original group set sail from Spain in June 1527 and landed near Tampa Bay, Florida, in April 1528. Narváez separated 300 men from the main group and began an overland expedition searching for the right spot to start a colony. Because of a mistake in his calculations, he led his men on a 1,500-mile (2,414 km) trek that ended when the group got stuck in northern Florida for several months. There, the Spanish explorers had to contend with hostile Indians and a lack of food. Now down to 250 men, they left on five barges built from wood, deerskin, horsehides (they killed their remaining horses for food and supplies), bits of trees, and their shirts and pants, which served as sails. They turned weapons into fittings for the boats. They were headed for Pánuco, the Spanish outpost settled by Cortés. After about a month of sailing along the coastline, the group ran into a terrible storm that separated the boats. Narváez told the men to "each do as he thought best to save himself."[3]

Cabeza de Vaca and about two dozen others landed on a small island off the western edge of Galveston Island. He named the island Malhado ("Isle of Misfortune"). The Indians there were the Karankawa. Cabeza de Vaca later described these Indian men as tall and strong with sugarcane piercing their nipples and lower lips. The women used Spanish moss or deerskin for skirts. They ate roots, fish, shellfish,

Cabeza de Vaca crosses the desert from Texas to Mexico. After landing on the Gulf Coast, Cabeza de Vaca spent years living among the local Indians, documenting their culture.

small animals, and the fruit of cactus plants. Stories exist that these Indians were cannibals, but Cabeza de Vaca's journal does not support that. Although they are extinct now, the Karankawa survived through the end of the Spanish colonial period, around 1800.

Cabeza de Vaca played various roles during the eight years he traveled around Texas and Mexico. For 18 months, he was held captive by the Mariame Indians. He was a slave of the Avavares for another eight months. Cabeza de Vaca also lived among the Coahuiltecans, a group of hunter-gatherer tribes in the region around San Antonio, for several years. For a time, he was respected as a medicine man and healer. In all, he identified and documented the lives of 23 separate tribes. He wrote about their daily lives; what they wore; what they ate; and how they celebrated, grieved, and interacted with each other and other tribes, both friend and foe. He described annual feasts and hunting methods.

It is believed the Apache arrived in southern Texas around the same time as the ill-fated Narváez expedition. They were seminomadic people, farming corn, beans, and squash for part of the year and following buffalo herds the rest of the year. Once they acquired enough horses from the Spanish, they became increasingly nomadic. They also ate horses when necessary, a habit the Spanish found distasteful. Indians and Spanish alike had to deal with natural challenges from scorpions, deadly spiders, rattlesnakes, mosquitoes, lack of food, and extreme weather such as drought, bitter cold, and searing heat.

Closer to the shoreline, the Atakapa Indians managed to survive in an area that was prone to flooding from the Gulf salt waters, making farming virtually impossible. As they moved slightly inland, certain crops were sometimes possible, but they relied on deer, bear, and occasionally bison for food. These Indians tattooed their faces and bodies. Both women and men wore little more than breechcloths around their waists, and they moved their settlements frequently.

The Indians never really had a chance against the Spaniards and the other Europeans who followed. Outnumbered, they fell to better weapons and the unfamiliar diseases the white men brought with them. Even the Tejas Indians, for whom the state of Texas was named, were relegated to reservations in the mid-1800s.

Cabeza de Vaca and three others survived an eight-year ordeal, traveling overland and finally ending up at Culiacán, a Spanish settlement near the Pacific coast of Mexico. Although Cabeza de Vaca explained where they landed and used landscape features to describe their journey, their exact route has never been pinpointed, although several historians and authors have published theories. He explored in the region of San Antonio, Goliad, and Laredo, and may have traveled as far south as Monterrey. The plants and animals were similar across this swath of Texas to what Santa Anna would have encountered on his various northern military campaigns.

Cabeza de Vaca wrote of the abundance of prickly pears, which can be eaten once the small, outer spines are removed. The red fruit, which is also commonly called "tuna," is ripe in summertime, when juice can be squeezed to drink. The outer peel, or pad, is dried in the sun to eat later. Cabeza de Vaca's account of the prickly pear shows the detailed way in which he wrote of his experiences in this strange, new world.

> This is a fruit that is of the size of an egg, and they are red and black and of very good flavor. They eat them three months of the year, in which they eat nothing else, because at the time they gathered them there came to them other Indians from farther on who brought bows, to trade and barter with them.[4]

The men learned how to survive by eating like the Indians they came in contact with. They dug roots and caught fish. They also enjoyed snakes, lizards, mice, insects, frogs, and deer. The hardy and drought-resistant mesquite trees, or shrubs, were common and were utilized both for their wood and for the bean pods they produced, which were dried and used as flour. When rain was plentiful, Indians raised corn, beans, pumpkins, and watermelons in the fertile soil.

Andrés Dorantes de Carranza (commonly called "Dorantes") was one of the four Spaniards who survived to tell about their experiences. He wrote:

> Inland are many deer, birds, and beasts. Cattle come as far as here. . . . They have small horns . . . the hair is very long and woolly like a rug. Of the smaller hides the Indians make blankets, and of the larger they make shoes and bucklers . . . the people descend on and live upon them.[5]

Dorantes was actually talking about buffalo, which provided food, shelter, and clothing for many of the Indians. He also called them "hunch-backed cows."

After returning to Spain in 1536, Cabeza de Vaca wrote a journal about his experiences and the animals, plants, and indigenous people he came across. It was published by the royal court of Spain in 1542 and called *Relación de los naufragios* (*Account of the Shipwreck*). With the other three survivors, Cabeza de Vaca was the first non-Indian to cross the continent. His co-survivors were Dorantes and his African slave, Estevanico, and Alonso Castillo Maldonado.

European interest in that region subsided for more than a century, growing again when the French explorer René-Robert Cavalier, sieur de La Salle (known as Robert de La Salle), brought settlers for a colony on the coast. Missionaries were sent to convert the Indians to Christianity and also to teach them Spanish laws. The soldiers who came along to protect the missionaries often brought their wives and children, settling the wild land with forts and villages.

In 1803, the U.S. government bought 828,800 acres (335,403 ha) from France. The land extended from what is now Arkansas west to Colorado, and north/south from Canada to Louisiana. Called the Louisiana Purchase, it opened up vast new frontiers for Easterners. This land did not include Texas, however, meaning anyone wishing to settle in that region needed permission from Spain, which still owned that area. In 1820, Virginian Moses Austin obtained such permission from the Spaniards to bring settlers into the area. He was given 200,000 acres (80,937 ha) on which to settle 300 families. Unfortunately, he died in 1821, right before the settlers were going to make their move. His son, Stephen, followed his father's dying request to settle the area, and carried out his plans. This was the same year that the Mexicans won their independence from Spain.

The Spanish were threatened by Austin's settlement and sent Catholic missionaries to the region accompanied by

Misión San Antonio de Valero served settlers and Indians for decades until the Spanish cavalry moved in and renamed it the Alamo. The mission was the site of Santa Anna's great victory over the Texas rebels.

soldiers for protection and to keep order. Thirty-six missionary settlements were established to convert the Indians, help Spanish settlements thrive, and keep others out. The landscape of northern Mexico and around San Antonio was similar to that of Spain, and so the Spaniards were comfortable there. They were used to ranching and subsisting in an area with little rainfall. But they were not used to the extreme drops in temperature that were possible during the winter months, when cold winds blew down from Canada. During the winter, hail and freezing rain were common. And during the summer months, occasional periods of high temperatures made the Spaniards' lives uncomfortable, as did the swarms of mosquitoes along the coast.

One of the early missions was Misión San Antonio de Valero, built on the banks of the San Antonio River, where San Antonio, Texas, is located today. Construction began in 1724, and the mission served settlers and the local Indians for about 70 years. In the early 1800s, Spain established a cavalry unit there, and the soldiers called the former mission "Alamo," Spanish for "cottonwood," which grew around the buildings.

The mission/fort and the town of San Antonio would come to play a large role in the struggle for Mexican independence from Spain and later in the war between Texas and Mexico. Santa Anna would realize one of the largest roles of his career and life in this southern Texas town: first experiencing a resounding victory over Texan rebels at the Alamo, then shortly thereafter, a humiliating defeat nearby.

Santa Anna's Early Career

Santa Anna joined the army two and a half months before the Mexican War of Independence started in 1810. It ended nine years later, and by then he was a battle-hardened colonel of 27. Although Santa Anna spent his youth fighting Indians and his fellow Mexicans, these battles took place mostly far away from his hometown. The war did not affect Xalapa or Veracruz terribly, aside from a few small skirmishes. He was not involved in any of the war's key battles either. He had been assigned to remote provinces in Mexico and also in Texas, where he got his first glimpse of the land that would play such a pivotal role in his career.

Santa Anna's minimal involvement in the war for independence helped him later in gaining support from all Mexicans; he had no wartime behavior to live down. He initially believed in the cause of the royalists—those who believed Mexico should remain a territory of Spain. Over time, however, he

Father Miguel Hidalgo y Costilla issues the battle cry during the Mexican War of Independence in this mural created by Juan O'Gorman. Although he wasn't a key player in the war, Santa Anna did gain valuable experience fighting in it, and he learned about other regions of Mexico.

reversed his opinion and joined the insurgency, made up of rebels devoted to gaining independence.

Santa Anna first served with the Fixed Infantry Regiment of Veracruz until April 1821. He was based initially at the port of Veracruz, along with many other locals who were immune to yellow fever. A great feeling of camaraderie developed among these men, and many of them went on to serve under Santa Anna in later years.

A few weeks after he turned 17, he was ordered to join a convoy north to end several Indian rebellions. His regiment set sail on March 13, 1811, with about 500 other troops under the command of Colonel Joaquín de Arredondo y Mioño, a headstrong but successful leader. By 1817, Arredondo and his troops had destroyed the Indians, put down the earliest rebellion in Texas, and won other battles. His ruthlessness was well known; he routinely had all prisoners executed, regardless of promises to spare them. Santa Anna seemed to have used Arredondo as a role model, both on the battlefield, where they showed no mercy, as well as off, where they each had a reputation as ladies' men and practical jokers.

Santa Anna's first experience in battle was in April 1811 in Aguayo (Ciudad Victoria, today), a town held by rebels. His battalion then defeated other rebel forces in two battles in May. These first three events earned Santa Anna the attention of his superior officers, and he was cited for distinguished service on the battlefield.

Santa Anna came to be known for his determination, high energy, and stubbornness. He may have picked up these traits from serving with Arredondo, who continued to push his men from one battle to the next, vanquishing insurgent bands at every opportunity. During one of these skirmishes, this time against the Indians in the region of Amoladeras at the end of August 1811, Santa Anna received his first battle wound when an arrow pierced his left hand. He continued to fight Indians for another 18 months, in the Sierra Gorda region. He was promoted to lieutenant by his eighteenth birthday and was entrusted with minor commands.

The Battle of Medina, August 18, 1813, won Santa Anna his first medal. This battle was particularly bloody, as the Texan rebel army, consisting of about 1,400 men, was outnumbered by Arredondo's 1,830 troops. After four hours of fighting, most of the rebel forces were dead. Those who had not been killed on the battlefield were shot later that day. None were spared. Arredondo's Spanish royalist troops then moved 20 miles (32.19 km) to San Antonio de Bexar, where they killed anyone suspected of rebel activity.

Santa Anna's attachment to Texas began during this campaign. He had experienced the beauty and vastness of this region and felt its allure. He wrote about "the beauty of this country which surpasses all description; with hills covered in grass, oak forests, and in the early evening one of the loveliest arrays that can be observed in the heavens."[6] He experienced his earliest victories there and carried fond memories of them; all this came into play during the 1835 revolution, when he took the Texans' rebellion personally.

One of the first events to try his honor and integrity happened after the battle at Medina. During a lull in fighting, Santa Anna began to play cards and gamble. After losing a large amount of money during one game, he forged two signatures (including that of General Arredondo) to withdraw funds from the troop's "bank" to pay his debt. When he was discovered, he claimed he was helping another officer and by doing so maintained the troop's honor. He paid the debt by borrowing 300 pesos and selling his fancy sword and everything he owned, except for two sets of clothes. He was never punished for the crime.

In November 1815, one year after his mother had died, 21-year-old Santa Anna was sent back to Veracruz, where a new governor recently had been installed. Don José García Dávila was the official who had allowed an underage Santa Anna to enroll in the army as a favor to his mother. Now he took the young man in and made him a close aide. They worked well together. Santa Anna said Dávila was like a father to him, and the older man praised Santa Anna in his reports to his superiors in Mexico City.

By all accounts, at this time, Santa Anna was a brave risk taker. He was ambitious and bright, willing to work hard to achieve his goals. He was not against stretching the truth to get his way, and he utilized every possible connection made by his well-known family. Some of the older soldiers seemed jealous of Santa Anna's rapid rise in the ranks. Those in Veracruz, especially, may have felt he had been given too much responsibility in that region. Santa Anna was not above pulling strings and going around those in command who disagreed with him. This direct approach was how he made friends with Viceroy Juan Ruiz de Apodaca, the official who governed New Spain in the name of Spain.

That friendship served Santa Anna well in November 1818 when he captured a rebel leader, Francisco de Asís, and had him publicly executed without the opportunity to surrender. Ignacio Cincunegui, a higher-ranking officer in the region who hated Santa Anna, reported him and demanded his suspension. Santa Anna immediately headed to Mexico City to argue his case before Apodaca. Santa Anna claimed that Asís deserved to be executed and claimed that he was close to capturing another insurgent leader but could not complete this mission if he were suspended. Several military men and priests from Veracruz intervened. General Pascual Liñán described Santa Anna as "active, zealous, indefatigable in his service, and of very good military knowledge." He excused some of his overzealousness because of his youth, saying, "it is not strange that on some occasions he may have exceeded his powers."[7] Viceroy Apodaca returned his command, and Santa Anna returned to duty.

FROM SOLDIER TO COMMUNITY BUILDER

Throughout 1819 and 1820, Santa Anna was given the very different task of building up communities, rather than tearing them down. He was appointed by Liñán, who was now the governor of Veracruz, to organize and reestablish the towns of Medellín, San Diego, Tamarindo, and Xamapa and to start a new one of Loma de Santa María, populating it with more than

300 insurgents who had received amnesty. He was appointed governor of these towns, where he managed the 593 families well. He became a popular man because he had plots of land to give away, and he gave them to rebels who surrendered to him.

His responsibilities as administrator were many: He planned the communities, overseeing construction and micromanaging everything from building design to what crops the farmers should grow. He found teachers for the schools and ensured the budgets included money for churches and shops to be built. He was given vast power, which he seemed to have handled well. He formed a royalist militia and forced all men between age 16 and 50 to serve; each family was ordered to grow extra food to feed the protectors. He had large structures built in each community in which soldiers could take refuge in case of a siege. He also kept records of the movements of all residents: No one could leave or enter without the approval of the community commander. He kept tight control over his towns. And they flourished and grew, peacefully, under his rule. According to historian Christon Archer, these villages became models of constructive counterinsurgency planning and established Santa Anna as a regional leader with a significant following outside the port city.

By the summer of 1820, the town council of Veracruz asked the governor for help against Santa Anna's tyrannical ways. They said he forced men to build private houses for the officers; charged them exorbitant prices for hay; and put people in jail for little or no cause. Governor Dávila, Santa Anna's friend, did remove him from office as the leader of San Diego, but never charged him with any wrongdoing. In 1821, after successfully leading expeditions against rebels and capturing large stores of weapons, Santa Anna was promoted to lieutenant colonel.

SANTA ANNA CHANGES SIDES

Until just after Santa Anna's twenty-seventh birthday, he remained a fervent royalist, loyal to Spain. On February 24,

IMMORTALIZING A FAMOUS BATTLE

Many artists attempted to re-create the battle scene at the Alamo. One of those painters, Henry Arthur McArdle (1836–1908), not only created one of the most detailed works, but also got General Santa Anna, who was 80 years old at the time the painting was made, to comment on the event.

McArdle did extensive research before painting *Dawn at the Alamo*. He found out what the equipment and uniforms looked like and what the landscape around the town had been. He looked up photos and paintings of the famous people involved in the siege and battle so he could accurately represent them.

According to writer Janey Levy, McArdle used a bit of creative license in his rendering. The large painting (7 feet by 12 feet, or 2.13 m by 3.66 m) hangs in the Senate Chamber in the Texas Capitol today.

> McArdle used light to draw special attention to William Barret Travis, David Crockett, and James Bowie and presented them in heroic poses. . . . The artist also made the three heroes handsome. In contrast, the Mexican soldiers have coarse, heavy, exaggerated features and assume poses that are definitely not heroic.

Levy, Janey. *The Alamo: A Primary Source History of the Legendary Texas Mission.* New York: Rosen Publishing Group, Inc., 2003. p. 53.

1821, a major event took place that changed Santa Anna's allegiance. By this time, both sides in the war for independence were tired of fighting. They realized that there would be no peace until independence was gained, so the leaders came to an agreement known as the Plan of Iguala, proposed by the head of the royalists, Agustín de Iturbide (known as El Libertador), and the rebel leader Vicente Guerrero. The agreement made three promises: Roman Catholicism would be the state religion; Mexico would be recognized as an independent country;

and all ethnicities would be recognized as being equal, ensuring they could live in the country safely.

On learning of the Plan of Iguala, Santa Anna changed sides and supported the cause of independence, which was

Agustín de Iturbide (*above*) led the coalition that ended the War of Independence. He briefly reigned as emperor of Mexico, and he is responsible for promoting Santa Anna to the post of brigadier general.

seen as a betrayal by those royalists who had supported and helped him. Thousands of royalists did the same thing, though, including his family, whose businesses had suffered during more than a decade of war. This was a confusing time, with former royalists and longtime insurgents fighting side by side. Over several months, Santa Anna led troops along the coast and into the mountains, where he continued to fight in his customary energetic style, but now on the side of independence. He was recognized for his efforts by Iturbide and appointed the commander general of the Veracruz province. Santa Anna also liberated Xalapa from royalist defenders in late May and promptly declared himself commander general there as well.

POPULIST LEADER

He used his popularity wisely and gained the support of both rich and poor by protecting the businesses of the former and reducing taxes on the latter. He did add some taxes to help pay for the army's expenses, but these were aimed at the rich of the city. He rewarded those who were loyal to him with key positions. Because he acted like a leader, the people respected him as one.

At the end of June, Santa Anna gave a rousing speech about liberating Veracruz. He told the town council he was leaving and sent a letter to Iturbide. He did not wait for permission from anyone; he just gathered his men and marched down the mountain to the port. Once at the city, he sent messengers into town with letters proclaiming his intent to free the city from those who would continue to control it, meaning the Spanish. He claimed he did not want to hurt anyone; he simply wanted to liberate the town in the way in which he had freed Xalapa.

Governor Dávila gathered the troops of the city to fight off Santa Anna. He denounced Santa Anna, his former friend, as a young man who was treacherous and willing to sacrifice his countrymen for his own ambition. Santa Anna and his men attacked Veracruz shortly after midnight on July 7, 1821. In pouring rain, they marched to the town center, where bitter fighting ensued for three hours. The royalists pushed Santa Anna's fighters out of town, and they retreated to Córdoba. At this time, the final treaty recognizing Mexico as independent from Spain was signed, creating a constitutional monarchy, one in which a king or queen rules the country according to a set of laws. The Treaties of Córdoba were signed on August 24 by Iturbide and the Spanish representative, Juan O'Donojú. In return for its independence, Iturbide promised that the Mexican throne would be given to a member of the Bourbon family, a European royal family.

MASTER OF PUBLIC RELATIONS

Santa Anna was a master of positive public relations. He was close friends with José María Tornel y Mendívil, a middle-class Veracruzano who was born in Orizaba, Xalapa's rival for the trade route to Mexico City. The two men became fast friends and remained friends for more than 30 years, sharing ambitions and similar tastes. Tornel was an excellent writer, and many of Santa Anna's pronouncements, letters, and speeches are thought to have been written by his friend. Known as a Santanista for his extreme loyalty to Santa Anna, Tornel is considered to be responsible for the general's rise to power over and over again, in spite of his responsibility for major defeats in 1836 and 1847. Some of Tornel's earliest writings speak of Santa Anna as a hero, a brave and moderate man, a man of the people who cared only for freedom from despotism for his countrymen. Both men realized that, with independence, the old rules no longer existed, and they proceeded to operate according to their own desires, making up the rules as they went along. Santa Anna's network of friends, his charm, and his cunning, along with Tornel's compelling written arguments in his favor, all helped propel Santa Anna to become the popular leader of the province of Veracruz.

GENERAL SANTA ANNA

In 1822, Iturbide declared himself emperor of Mexico and promoted Santa Anna to brigadier general. The two men had become estranged for various reasons over the previous year, and each was jockeying to win a popularity contest among the people. Santa Anna continued to win that title in his home province of Veracruz, and by December of that year, he instigated a revolt against Iturbide, using the argument that absolute rule was not good for the country. He argued that the country should be a republic, governed by a congress and the laws of a constitution.

A series of revolts around the country led to the agreement called the Plan of Casa Mata, signed on Februry 1, 1823. In less than two months, the terms of the plan had reached all areas of the country, with almost everyone in agreement. This consensus led Iturbide to abdicate his throne, restore the Congress, and return to Europe. By April, most of the country backed Santa Anna's view that a republican government was the most beneficial for the country. His leadership of the revolt against the monarchy gave him reason to declare himself the founder of the republic, and he was recognized as such by many. Santa Anna was not yet 30 years old, and he had accomplished so much.

5

A New Republic

The new constitution adopted on October 4, 1824, was the first set of laws enacted for the Republic of Mexico. It established Mexico as a federalist republic, a group of states governed by representatives of the people, with Roman Catholicism as the official religion. This document was similar to the Spanish constitution of 1812, with a strong legislative branch that elected the president. It also contained elements similar to those in the U.S. Constitution.

This document was important to the development of the Texas territory because it promised freedoms the settlers could not find elsewhere. The liberal social conditions found in the Texas territory continued to attract increasing numbers of Americans and Europeans. The settlers lived peacefully under this form of government until 1835, when President Santa Anna dissolved the constitution of 1824 and replaced it with the more stringent constitution of 1835, which removed many of the political and social freedoms the settlers had enjoyed. Instead of the states holding power, power was once again centralized in Mexico City. These changes prompted the revolts in Texas and led to the Mexican-American War.

José Miguel Ramón Adaucto Fernández y Félix became the first Mexican president in 1824, after the overthrow of the emperor. He chose the common name of Guadalupe Victoria in gratitude to Catholic icon Our Lady of Guadalupe, and Victoria, which means "victory." During his tenure, which ended in 1829, Victoria abolished slavery and established the Military Academy. Victoria's presidency was a time of transition, as the country grew accustomed to its new government. Hopes were high for a period of peace and enlightenment. Freedom of the press was granted in the new constitution, and there were expanded educational opportunities for the country's children. Victoria was revered by the Mexican people and named *Benemérito de la Patria* ("Hero of the Country") by the Mexican congress after he died in 1843.

During Victoria's presidency, Santa Anna settled into the area between Xalapa and Veracruz, where he bought the hacienda Manga de Clavo. He gained regional prestige and was appointed governor from 1827 to 1829, further cementing his position in the region. He continued to write and speak on behalf of a strong federal republic, and although some have claimed he had plans to declare himself absolute ruler of Mexico, that does not seem to be the case during this time. In fact, he took something of a break from life in the public eye between 1825 and 1827. He seemed content to spend his time running his hacienda. He had also recently been married to a young woman from an influential Spanish family. Eventually, Santa Anna was the major landowner in the areas of Xalapa and Veracruz, providing jobs to many residents of the area and growing most of the region's produce and cattle. It was during this time that Santa Anna became the caudillo of Veracruz—a man of power and influence.

His purchase of Manga de Clavo and increasing success as a landowner helped build his authority locally. The immense estate (somewhere between 46 and 70 square miles, or 119 sq. km and 181 sq. km, depending on the source) was located outside Veracruz. He spent most of his time between 1825 and 1842 there; that is, when he was not off leading the army; personally overseeing his land, livestock, and tenants; and running all aspects of the hacienda. His home was situated far from Mexico City, which he detested, but on the main road between the capital and Veracruz, allowing him to be aware of important visitors to the region. He gradually added land to his original holdings, becoming the largest landowner in the state of Veracruz.

PERSONAL LIFE

His first wife, María Inés de la Paz García, was 14 when they married in 1825. He married her in absentia, meaning he was not present at the ceremony. Instead, her father stood in for the groom. It would seem that Santa Anna was interested in his new wife mainly because of her rich and influential family

THE PEOPLE

The following terms are used in this book as descriptors for some of the settlers of Texas and Mexico:

Tejano—Identifies those in Texas who were of Mexican or Central American descent.

Texian—The name Texas revolutionaries gave themselves. They were not Texans or Tejanos, rather they were *Texians* as a way to differentiate themselves.

Criollo—A person of pure Spanish blood who lived in Mexico.

Mestizo—People of mixed European and Latin American ancestry.

and how it could help him politically. Her dowry, or marriage gift to him, was enough to help him buy the hacienda and 100 head of cattle shortly after the wedding.

The couple had four children together—Guadalupe, María del Carmen, Manuel, and Antonio. However, Santa Anna also had many extramarital affairs and fathered at least four children with other women. He acknowledged these four in his last will; however, three more have been found by biographers, and others also may exist. His wife was only 33 when she died of pneumonia in 1844. His popularity had apparently rubbed off onto her, or she somehow earned her own version of national respect, since a large funeral procession was held before her burial, and days of national mourning were observed.

BACK TO POLITICS

Santa Anna once again gained the public's attention when he became governor of Veracruz from the end of January until early September 1828. During this time, he actively promoted commerce around the region, instituting trade fairs. He also strengthened police forces and ended assaults by banditos, or outlaws. Roads were repaired and cleaned up, and an irrigation project was begun. He kept close watch on the province's finances and personally oversaw political appointments. He backed educational reforms and improvements, budgeting large sums of money to build and maintain new schools. His success in this region, combined with coming events, put him in a position to move again onto the national stage.

In January 1829, a former rebel leader and general, Vicente Ramón Guerrero Saldaña, became president. Guerrero had helped Santa Anna put down a coup attempt against President Victoria two years earlier, a fortuitous event for Santa Anna, who was confirmed as governor and commander general of Veracruz. Perhaps Santa Anna had matured enough to handle the position, evidenced by a speech he made to the citizens of Veracruz on February 10, 1829. In it, he stated four themes that

This oil painting shows Santa Anna defeating the Spanish at Tampico in 1829. Santa Anna's victory at Tampico made him a national hero.

he had upheld throughout his political life. He also presented himself as a Veracruzano, a man of the people of Veracruz, yet at the same time, as a hero of the state. He spoke with confidence and passion about Mexico's problems and stressed that they came from the behavior of the country's political parties, which could not get along, even to benefit Mexico. He said:

> My heart only seeks peace and unity. It joyfully gives in to the redeeming idea of a general and fraternal reconciliation; that the kiss of true peace among Mexicans of all parties, serves as the medicine which may cure all of our ills before they infect us. . . . The ridiculous names which have so far been given to

the parties tear the nation apart; let there be only one . . . the party of the true Mexican patriots. Let us prepare for a great national reconciliation, because only this will serve as the anchor of our hopes.[8]

On August 1, Santa Anna received word that Spanish troops were invading Mexico in Tampico, intent on repossessing former territory. He sailed for Tampico one week later and attacked on August 21. The Spanish troops thought they would be welcomed by Mexicans who had tired of independence; however, the truth was the opposite. After more than two weeks of waiting each other out, and occasional skirmishes, Santa Anna ordered an assault on the Spanish troops on September 10. The battle lasted for more than a day, until General Isidro Barradas surrendered and agreed to return to Cuba. News of Santa Anna's victory at Tampico swept Mexico, and he became a national hero. Everywhere he went, he was met with receptions, marching bands, and festivals. He was given awards and citations. He was named "favorite citizen" by the states of Jalisco and Zacatecas, and September 11 was declared a national holiday.

BACK TO THE HACIENDA

At the end of 1829, Santa Anna went into semi-retirement once again. He retreated to his hacienda, where he spent his time managing the estate, as he had four years earlier. He now had a growing family with whom he liked to spend his time. He had changed. Now he was a true hero, nationally as well as regionally, admired for securing independence for Mexico once and for all. For almost two years after Santa Anna returned to Manga de Clavo, General Anastasio Bustamante served as president, leading a traditionalist government that restricted states' powers and limited voting rights to male property owners. (Manuel Gómez Pedraza had actually won the election of 1828, but under military threat, he denounced his office and traveled to the United States, where he lived in exile in Pennsylvania.) The Banco de Avío was created in an attempt to boost the economy; former royalists made a comeback; and the administration became known for its repressive tendencies. Guerrero had been arrested and threatened with death; however, Santa Anna wrote to Bustamante urging him to spare the life of the ex-president, reminding him that Guerrero was godfather to his daughter, Guadalupe, but the letter arrived too late. Public opinion turned sharply against Bustamante after he approved the execution of Guerrero on February 14, 1831.

Santa Anna maintained his distance from Mexico City until he was asked in early January 1832 to join officials organizing a revolt against Bustamante's administration, and he took over as head of the revolutionaries on January 3, in Veracruz. He was still wildly popular there, even though he had been out of politics for about two years. In letters written to Bustamante and members of his cabinet and military commanders, Santa Anna called himself a mediator and suggested ways the current unrest could be brought to a peaceful resolution. He suggested the royalists in the cabinet be replaced with men who had a good national reputation. He assured Mexico City that the public and rebels would be satisfied if certain changes were made in the government.

SANTA ANNA'S MILITIAS

While he was making attempts to resolve issues, Santa Anna was utilizing his solid network of friends and allies in Veracruz who were willing to help him financially as well as strategically. On February 21, government soldiers under the command of General José María Calderón arrived outside the city. Within 10 days, Santa Anna got the report that this battalion was leaving for Puente to escape yellow fever at the port city. Santa Anna led about 1,400 men out of the city, caught up with the government troops and passed them, cutting them off at Tolome. Calderón, however, had a strong defense. The first Battle of the 1832 Civil War was fierce, and Santa Anna's rebel militias were defeated. Calderón could have solidified his victory by following Santa Anna's men to the port, where they had retreated; however, after two months in that region, Calderón had lost up to 1,000 men to yellow fever, and he stayed back.

At almost the same time, the cabinet members whose resignation Santa Anna had requested, resigned. But by then it was too late because the revolt had spread to other states. Santa Anna also demanded that President Bustamante resign. He asked for former president Manuel Gómez Pedraza to return from exile in the United States to complete his term.

This request seemed strange because Santa Anna had been part of the threat against Pedraza in 1828; however, he knew that by acting in this practical, constitutionally correct way, he would gain additional support of the people. According to author Will Fowler, this action "gave the rebellion a legitimacy it had originally lacked . . . he could claim he was returning Mexico to its former constitutional path."[9] Santa Anna knew that Pedraza had only a few months left in his term and could not be reelected. As these elements lined up, it became more likely that Santa Anna could become the next president.

Santa Anna and Calderón met on June 11 at El Encero, the hacienda near Xalapa that Santa Anna would eventually own. They were unable to come to an agreement, and Santa Anna continued to Orizaba with a contingent of 3,000 men. He sent another letter to Pedraza in Bedford Springs, Pennsylvania, explaining that additional Mexican states were in support of Pedraza's return. It was during this time that Santa Anna's sister, Francisca, was arrested and imprisoned, convicted of conspiring to overthrow the government by acting as an intermediary between her brother and the rebels. She was one of only a handful of women arrested for political reasons in the nineteenth century.

In mid-September, as he was marching to confront Bustamante's army, Santa Anna received word that Pedraza was returning to Mexico. The Battle of the Rancho de Posadas in Puebla on November 6 left no clear winner, and the two armies took turns retreating and attacking back and forth across Mexico until a last battle on December 23. After this fight, they sat down and signed the Treaty of Zavaleta, which ended the 1832 Civil War. This treaty agreed that Pedraza would be recognized as president until April 1, 1833; everyone involved with the revolt would be pardoned; and the current system of government would be maintained. This treaty was the precursor to Santa Anna's election as president in 1833. Santa Anna once again "retired" to his hacienda, where he waited, knowing he had an excellent chance at the presidency in the upcoming elections.

SANTA ANNA'S FIRST TERM AS PRESIDENT

Santa Anna's expectations were met, and he was elected to his first term; however, he was not present for the swearing-in. Instead, his vice president, Valentín Gómez Farías, took the oath of office for him on April 1, 1833. Santa Anna first arrived in Mexico City on May 15, although he did not stay long. He never lingered in the capital, preferring to leave most of the governance up to his vice president.

Santa Anna was president until 1836, but actually served for only a few months, preferring to spend his time tending to his hacienda or traveling around the country. He left the actual governing to his vice president. He did have an effect on the country's financial system, which he felt needed radical reform. Taxes instituted during two of his later terms (1841–1843 and 1853–1855) were his way of alleviating the government's lack of financial resources. He already agreed with the Congress's proposal to tax the Catholic Church, believing that it was the church's duty to help finance the government. He felt it was all right as long as these changes were made slowly, in order to avoid revolt. He also tried to reform the army, reducing its size.

It was during this first year of his first term that Santa Anna met with Stephen Austin in Mexico City on November 5. He

In 1833, Santa Anna (*above*) was named president of Mexico. Perhaps because of his experience as military commander, Santa Anna was often seen by the Mexican people as a dictator.

refused Austin's request for Texas's independence; however, he did give Austin permission to bring in more U.S. immigrants and to work toward reforms of the legal system in the province. Santa Anna's first presidency was marked by regular uprisings and revolts and attempts to cast him as supreme dictator of Mexico. He published a manifesto at the end of June claiming he was not interested in a dictatorship and reminding the country that he was the one who had pushed for a more liberal political system as far back as 1822. He wrote that he had faith in the Mexican people and their ability to be democratically governed.

PUTTING DOWN REBELLION

In the late summer of 1833, he led a large contingent of about 2,400 men northwest from Mexico City to control the rebels who were pushing for the abolition of the presidency. Santa Anna's men got out of the city just before it was hit by a devastating cholera epidemic. True to form, he used circumstances to bolster his actions—in this case, telling his men that their "heroism in pursuing the enemies of our laws and institutions became all the more pronounced during the time of cholera,"[10] thus invigorating them for the battle ahead. At several stops along the way, he gave rousing speeches exciting the men and getting them ready for battle to protect independence and the government. On October 7, his army attacked the rebel troops led by General Mariano Arista and overran the city of Guanajuato. The fight was over within a couple of hours, with Arista soundly beaten. Santa Anna addressed the citizens of Guanajuato, inviting them to happily celebrate their renewed freedom.

A tug-of-war between reformists, extremists, and moderates (with behind-the-scenes maneuverings) was constant throughout his presidency. Although Santa Anna's cabinet was staffed with men who shared his ideas of reform, the Congress was confrontational in its demands, and public opinion was split down the middle. Almost exactly two years after taking office, Santa Anna published another manifesto in which he said he had been elected to "contain or moderate precipitated decisions or excessive passion ... he promised to defend religion, liberty, security, and all the rights guaranteed by the Constitution."[11] Congress ignored his request for a special meeting on May 21, 1834, and a few days later, the Plan of Cuernavaca was proclaimed by Tornel, Santa Anna's minister of war. The plan had five main points: (1) All decrees issued against individuals and the church and in favor of Masonic sects were abolished; (2) All laws violating the constitution and the general will were reversed; (3) Santa Anna was to be given the authority to execute these demands; (4) All deputies who favored these reforms were removed from office; (5) Santa Anna would have forces in favor of the plan at his service to ensure it was carried out. The plan was highly popular and endorsed by the public, the army, town councils, and various other governmental bodies.

This plan allowed Santa Anna to shut down the Congress and reverse many of the laws it had passed and to fire his vice president. He was supported by the church and many officers as well as businessmen. But despite what many thought at the time, he did not take the opportunity to proclaim himself dictator. Once he believed the country was again on a steady course, led by his new cabinet and Congress, he left for Manga de Clavo on January 28, 1835, leaving the government to be run by his new vice president, Miguel Barragán.

By the end of the year, Santa Anna was out of retirement and back in the saddle, headed for the province of Texas, which was in revolt against the Mexican government. Most American Texans did not want to learn Spanish, live by Mexican laws, and convert to Catholicism, all rules the settlers were supposed to follow. After Mexico abolished slavery and then overthrew federalism early in 1835 (giving the territories less autonomy), the time was right for revolt. Santa Anna did not have to lead forces into the remote province, but he preferred the hazards of the battlefield to those of the capital city.

The Road
to the Alamo

The Mexican government hoped to fill the Texas territory with their citizens, but few wanted to move, so Mexican leaders decided to invite in people from other countries, offering them tax-free residency for 10 years. All the immigrants had to do to get land—for only about 12 cents per acre—was to agree to convert to Catholicism and swear allegiance to Mexico. Land was fertile, and people felt they could make good lives in Mexico. Before long, those born in the territory outnumbered the Tejanos—the residents born in Mexico. One of the groups of settlers was led by Stephen Austin, Moses's son, who followed his father's plan and built the colony of San Felipe near the Brazos River, not far from Houston. Eventually, that town was overrun and burned by Santa Anna's advancing army in 1836.

By 1830, American immigrants outnumbered native Texans by 3 to 1. Many of these newer settlers never agreed to obey the Mexican laws. They refused to convert and smuggled in goods. As the population grew, the U.S. government offered to buy Texas from Mexico, which refused. Instead, Mexico passed a new law limiting how many settlers could enter from the United States, while allowing an increasing number of settlers to come in from Europe. The Mexican government tightened its control of the region, and settlers lost some of their rights. These settlers named themselves "Texians" and formed two political parties. Those in the War Party were bitter and angry; declared they could govern themselves; and agitated for independence. The Peace Party remained loyal to the Mexican government. William Travis was a member of the first group. Steve Austin, however, belonged to the Peace Party, and was well known and had many friends. In addition to his position as a legislator in the Mexican government in Texas, he started the first militia in the area to protect the settlers from Indian raids. This "police force" later became the Texas Rangers.

In 1835, Austin joined a delegation carrying a draft constitution proclaiming Texas a free and independent entity. The men had planned to meet with President Santa Anna; however, he was away, and so they met with the acting president, Vice President Gómez Farías, who turned down their request. Austin wrote to friends in Texas, agreeing that the time had come to declare independence. When the letter was intercepted, Austin was jailed; troops were sent to Texas, the Texas legislature was disbanded, and the delegates were arrested.

President Santa Anna sent one of his trusted commanders, General Martín Perfecto de Cos, to the Texas frontier to get the settlers under control. Cos dispersed his troops, sending some to the town of Gonzales to take its cannon. But the townspeople refused to give it up, believing Santa Anna was trying to make them vulnerable. Instead, they buried it in an orchard to keep it out of Mexican hands. The ensuing battle, on October 2, 1835, was the first battle of the Texas War for Independence. The first shot was called the "Texas shot heard 'round the world." Cos was kept at bay, and he retreated to San Antonio. Austin declared war on October 4, and volunteers came, including Colonel Jim Bowie, Colonel Jim Fannin, and Colonel William Travis. A week later, this so-called Army of

Stephen Austin (*above*) is known as the Father of Texas, and the state capital is named for him. Austin brought 300 families from the United States to colonize Texas.

the People left for San Antonio, where General Cos waited. Outside San Antonio, the two sides took turns attacking and retreating for almost two months, with neither side able to claim success. Additional American troops joined the Texas rebels, enabling them to defeat Cos, who surrendered and promised to leave Texas forever.

THE SIEGE OF THE ALAMO

Meanwhile, Santa Anna's army had marched long and hard to reach its goal. The date was February 23, 1836, and a Texan scout rode into the town of San Antonio de Bexar to warn the citizens: Mexican general Antonio López de Santa Anna was only eight miles outside the town with thousands of troops!

As the townspeople evacuated, Lieutenant Colonel William Travis, the co-commander of the Texas troops, sent Dr. John Sutherland to climb the tower of the San Fernando Church, the tallest building in the town. Sutherland could see for miles from his perch, but nothing was visible except the vast, rolling prairie. Travis left a guard there with orders to ring the church bell if he saw anything. Sutherland and John Smith, a soldier familiar with the region, went to scout the area on horseback. They told Travis that they would ride back quickly if they saw signs of the enemy; otherwise, they would walk their horses back, as a signal that all was well. Within 2 miles (3.2 km) of the village, the two scouts spotted the advancing line of the Mexican army; their first estimate was 1,500 troops. The two men turned and rode back into town, and the tower guard rang the church bell.

Since there was nowhere for the Texan troops to go, they retreated into the Alamo, the former mission. Its walls would provide the best defense the town had to offer. Others hurried there for protection, including Susanna Dickinson, wife of Captain Almeron Dickinson, and their baby daughter, Angelina; another soldier's wife, Ana Esparza, and their four children; Petra Gonzales, who was very old; and several black slaves. More than a dozen women and children joined the soldiers in the fort, but there was no listing of the civilians, so an accurate count is impossible.

The mission-turned-fort covered 3 acres (1.2 ha) of land. Stone walls about 4 feet (1.2 m) wide and 9 to 12 feet (2.74 m to 3.66 m) high surrounded a rectangular courtyard of 154 yards by 54 yards (140.8 m by 49.38 m). On the north and west sides, small, adobe rooms lined the walls. A long, one-story building called the Long Barracks ran along the south wall, with the 10-foot-wide (3 m) main entrance nearby. The southeast side of the compound had a gap in the wall; other areas of the walls were incomplete or weak. In early February, only 120 men were there, not nearly enough to defend it well. William Travis showed up with 30 men, which still was not enough. He had hoped to have 1,000 soldiers, but there was no money to pay them or to buy them food or clothes. But the Alamo and San Antonio were important for the defense of Texas because they blocked one of the two main roads into the region from the south.

Jim Bowie, who made the Bowie knife famous, was the other Texan commander. Two of his sisters-in-law joined the group inside the fort. Bowie and a group of soldiers quickly searched the town, retrieving whatever supplies they could find, knowing they soon would be surrounded and trapped inside. They brought back sacks of grain, guns, and even cows. Fewer than 200 Texas rebel-soldiers were inside the fort to defend it and the villagers. These men were prepared to fight and determined not to surrender.

Riders were sent out with pleas for help. Jim Bonham rode to Goliad, about 95 miles (153 km) away, bringing a message to Colonel James Fannin, asking him to bring his 450 troops immediately. Sutherland, who had fallen off his horse and injured his hip while out on his original scouting mission, rode 60 miles (96.56 km) east to the town of Gonzales, in search of volunteers.

The gates to the courtyard were pulled closed, and none too soon. The Mexican army arrived shortly thereafter, led by a band and standard-bearers, the men who carried the flags.

The cavalry (soldiers on horseback) arrived first, followed by the infantry, or the men on foot. Mexican soldiers unfurled a red flag in the church tower, only about 800 yards (732 m) from the Alamo's walls. The defenders knew the flag sent a message of "no quarter," meaning the Mexican troops would show no mercy to those within the walls.

SANTA ANNA'S REVENGE

After General Cos was defeated at San Antonio, Santa Anna decided to teach the Texans a lesson. As the president of Mexico and the army's commander in chief, he did not have to lead the attack against the Texan rebels, but he wanted to destroy them. He was not only angry over their traitorous behavior toward Mexico; he felt personally betrayed. He believed the Texans were squatters, living in Mexican territory illegally and claiming large pieces of land while ignoring the laws of his country and of the church. Santa Anna was 42 years old at the time and was not a big man, standing about 5 feet 10 inches (177.8 centimeters). But he had big plans and patterned himself after his hero, Napoléon Bonaparte, even dressing in a similar uniform—a red and black jacket full of medals. Dressed this way, with a dark, intense stare and slick, black hair, he did resemble Napoléon. In fact, he often called himself "Napoléon of the West."

In preparation for the march into Texas, Santa Anna accepted donations from friends and the church and took out personal loans to finalize his plans. He ordered thousands of pounds of hardtack (hard, dry biscuits), recruited more soldiers, gathered horses for the cavalry, and found carts with oxen and mules. Many of the new soldiers were Maya Indians from southern Mexico who did not even speak Spanish. Santa Anna had no choice; to fight he would need to impress, or kidnap, soldiers. He planned to mix these new recruits with experienced soldiers to create a strong army.

He knew that the Texans would not expect him to make the northward trek before springtime, so he decided to leave as soon as possible, even though the threat of cold winter temperatures and nasty weather was real. Imagine 6,000 soldiers, some on horses, most on foot, wearing blue cotton uniforms and leather sandals or boots. Some wore tall, black hats with visors and plumes of feathers. The Indians and Mexicans who were not members of the official army wore loose, everyday clothing. They all set out toward the

IN SANTA ANNA'S WORDS

Santa Anna's reply to *Dawn at the Alamo* painter Henry Arthur McArdle, which is kept in the Texas State Library and Archives Commission, centers mainly on his belief that the behavior of the Texas rebels led to their slaughter; he was given no choice but to kill them all because they had been insulting and refused to surrender. He added that he had nothing of substance to add to his official reports made after the battle.

Dear Sir:
In response to your favor of the 4th of January, I have to say that in regard to the capture or restoration of the fortress of the Alamo, in April 1836, there is but little I can add to what was said in my official dispatches, and what was common knowledge. Notwithstanding, for your satisfaction, I will add that, that conflict of arms was bloody, because the chief Travis, who commanded the forces of the Alamo, would not enter into any settlement, and his responses were insulting, which made it imperative to assault the fort before it could be reinforced by Samuel Houston who was marching to its aid with respectable forces. The obstinancy of Travis and his soldiers was the cause of the death of the whole of them, for not one would surrender. The struggle lasted more than two hours, and until the ramparts were resolutely scaled by Mexican soldiers.

Texas border, which was about 500 miles (805 km) away. The weather turned bad almost immediately. The temperature dropped, and a cold wind brought heavy rain and snow. The cotton clothing was inadequate, especially for the Maya, who were used to tropical temperatures. Most of them did not even have tents.

ARRIVAL IN THE VILLAGE

Santa Anna divided the large army into units that marched out several days apart so that supplies could be distributed more easily. This organization created difficulty in communication, however, and required the various commanders to be very cooperative. The troops moved steadily, without much sleep or food. Many died, but they kept moving. The journey took about six weeks. Water was scarce for the men and animals, and also for the women and children who accompanied their soldier husbands and fathers on the journey. On February 21, the army reached the Medina River, about 25 miles (40 km) from San Antonio, where they rested for two days. While they were there, a small group of white men approached, waving a red, white, and green flag that had two stars in the center, one for Texas and the other representing the Mexican state of Coahuila. The men appealed to Santa Anna for a peaceful settlement, but the general ignored them and sent them away. The Mexicans entered San Antonio on February 23, waving flags with the large eagle emblem for the Mexican central government.

Within minutes of the Mexicans' arrival in the town's plaza, the Texans fired an 18-pound (8.2 kg) cannonball. The shot showed the Mexicans that the rebels were serious, but Bowie still sent a note asking for peace talks. Santa Anna's return message was curt; he would not discuss any terms. Travis also sent a messenger asking to talk with the Mexicans, but Colonel Juan Almonte replied that there would be no compromise and ordered the Texans to surrender or die. When Travis got this message, he answered by firing the cannon again.

Santa Anna leads his ill-equipped, ill-clad army on a killing march across the frozen plains of Coahuila. The commander was heading north to bring Texas back under Mexican control.

As his men got settled in the town and around the Alamo, Santa Anna chose his headquarters. A small, one-story building with a flat roof allowed him to keep a close watch on the proceedings within the town without being too close to the center. Throughout that first night, Texan messengers snuck in and out, heading for Goliad and Gonzales for help and for supplies. The Mexican army had not all arrived yet.

The Mexican soldiers dug trenches, placed three cannons around the perimeter of the Alamo's walls, and erected other defensive barriers. Inside the Alamo, Jim Bowie had been very sick for a week, with what may have been typhoid fever. He had turned over full command to Travis, who ordered men to dig trenches inside the plaza, erect structures to hold cannons, and patch holes in the walls. The women and children huddled inside the church's small rooms. The messenger returned from Goliad with a message that help was on its way. Travis sent another messenger out with an urgent plea for reinforcements, writing, "I shall never surrender or retreat." He signed it, "in victory or death," and his name.

PRELIMINARY FIGHTING BEGINS

At midmorning on February 25, about 200 Mexican soldiers attacked the Alamo. The defenders fired back with cannon, rifles, muskets, shotguns, and pistols. The soldiers retreated to small huts near the walls for cover. That night Travis sent out a few of his men to torch the huts, which burned to the ground. He also dispatched a messenger to General Sam Houston asking for reinforcements.

The next day the Mexican cavalry attacked the rear of the compound, and again they were turned back. Later that day, another Mexican unit arrived with more cannons, which now were trained on three sides of the fort. The Mexicans cut off the Texans' water supply from a nearby irrigation ditch. Jim Bowie was carried outside on his cot, and he encouraged the soldiers to stay strong and keep fighting, no matter what. Late in the afternoon, Santa Anna was fired at by one of the defenders as he walked about inspecting his troops. The house he was using as a command post also was fired on, but sustained no damage.

Late that night, 32 volunteers from Gonzales arrived. These men were not even soldiers; they were farmers and businessmen who wanted to help turn the tide for Texas. Inside the Alamo, it was becoming increasingly difficult to hold out, faced with regular bombardment from the Mexican cannons. They were low on supplies, the walls were poor protection, and the compound was so large that the ranks of the defenders were stretched thin trying to protect it all.

The Mexicans were also low on food, and the resupply wagons were still heading north. In an excellent example of his boasting style, Santa Anna sent one messenger to the wagons, telling the drivers to hurry, and another to Mexico City, reporting on success in San Antonio, never mentioning the Texans who remained under siege in the mission/fort.

Travis sent one last letter to friends, asking them to care for his seven-year-old son. He gathered the men one more time and explained the choices they faced: surrender, escape, or fight to the death. Several sources tell the story of a line in the sand Travis supposedly drew with the toe of his boot. He told the men willing to fight with him to cross the line, and every one did except one. The story goes that even Bowie's cot was carried across the line. The one man who chose not to fight escaped the Alamo that night and disappeared.

In the meantime, Santa Anna was busy meticulously planning every detail of the final attack. He ordered soldiers around the perimeter to hold their posts and had others build support structures for the 12-pound (5.4 kg) cannons that were coming with the last Mexican contingent. He constantly rearranged the soldiers outside the walls, inching them forward bit by bit. He also had a Mexican band play loud music every night accompanied by shouting Mexican soldiers and gunshots, meant to deprive the rebels of sleep.

REINFORCEMENTS TURN BACK

Fannin, who had left Goliad with 330 men and four cannons, never made it to San Antonio. Unfortunately for the defenders, Santa Anna's scouts reported that reinforcements were on the way, and he sent troops to stop them. Fannin's men had already turned back after three wagons broke down. Also, the San Antonio River was swollen from recent storms, making crossing nearly impossible. As Colonel Fannin and his officers were trying to decide how to continue, scouts rode up reporting on the advancing Mexican troops. Fannin knew he had to go back to Goliad to protect the citizens there. The Alamo's last hope was gone.

On March 4, 1836, Santa Anna decided it was time to teach the rebels the lesson he had come to impart, but his generals were split in their opinions on the timing of the attack. Two of the four said to wait—they did not have adequate supplies, and they needed more doctors. They also knew the Texans had limited food, water, and ammunition, and asked Santa Anna to prolong the siege rather than attack. But Santa Anna was adamant and did not want to allow for rebel reinforcements to arrive. He ordered the men to prepare for an attack the next day.

The Alamo and San Jacinto

Santa Anna controlled every aspect of the assault on the Alamo. He ordered his chief of staff, Colonel Juan Almonte, to pass down the following orders: Soldiers were not allowed to smoke or speak while waiting for the signal to attack. They were to hold all fire until soldiers were on the ladders that would be placed against the walls. Once the bugle sounded the attack, they had to fire immediately, without stopping. Soldiers could not wear capes or coats. They had to wear shoes (many, especially the Indians, were unused to wearing shoes), and they had to tighten the chinstraps of their hats.

His plan was intricate. Mexican soldiers would prepare for the attack near the walls while it was still dark. Then at daybreak, four columns of soldiers would charge on foot simultaneously, while the cavalry would cover the east flank, stopping any Texan who tried to escape. Santa Anna himself would send in additional troops as needed. He believed that Mexico's

Santa Anna and his troops storm the Alamo on March 6, 1836, in this nineteenth-century engraving. Hundreds of Texas rebels were killed in battle or executed by the Mexicans, but Santa Anna's victory would prove to be short-lived.

honor was at stake, and he was ready to teach the men in the Alamo a lesson.

DAYBREAK

A Mexican bugle sounding the attack woke the people inside the Alamo's walls at 5:00 A.M. Instantly, they were at their posts and ready to fight back. Mexican soldiers swarmed the north wall first and were so close, so quickly, that the rebels' cannons were ineffective. William Travis was one of the first to die, shot in the head by a Mexican marksman. The Texians had lined up their guns so they could shoot one after another without reloading. So many Mexicans stormed the north wall that they were killed accidentally by their countrymen closing in behind them. Santa Anna was watching from his headquarters and was displeased with the confusion. He ordered in reserves led by officers to try to regain some control over the charge, as the Mexicans came at the walls in waves.

Davy Crockett and some of his Tennessee troops were on the south side. Enrique Esparza, a young boy inside the Alamo who survived the battle, wrote later about Crockett's brave fight: "Crocket was everywhere . . . and personally slew many of the enemy with his rifle, pistol, and his knife. He fought hand to hand. He clubbed his rifle when they closed in on him and knocked them down with its stock . . . he fought to his last breath . . . when he died there was a heap of slain (Mexican soldiers) in front and on each side of him. Those he had all killed before he finally fell on top of the heap."[12]

Many of the rebels went to the north wall to help their comrades, leaving other sections of the wall undefended and allowing the Mexicans a clear path in. Mexicans seized the 18-pound (8.2 kg) cannon and killed its crew. Many more Mexicans then swarmed into the courtyard. There were simply too many of them. Some of the rebels tried to escape, but the cavalry soldiers killed them all. The fighting occurred in close quarters; knives and bayonets were used in hand-to-hand combat. They also beat each other with their guns.

Then the Texans retreated to special rooms prepared for such an eventuality. The doors were blocked with earthen walls that were just high enough to allow the rebels to shoot at the Mexicans in the plaza. There was little protection out there, and many Mexicans were killed. Then the Mexicans shot at the defenders with the large cannon, breaking through the walls.

They swarmed in and engaged in more hand-to-hand combat. One Texan ran toward the gunpowder storage room with a torch, planning to blow everything up, but he was shot before he got there. The only rebels remaining at this point were Captain Almeron Dickinson and his crew with the 12-pound (5.4 kg) cannon. They mounted it on a high wall behind the chapel. He found his wife and kissed her good-bye, and was killed soon thereafter, along with his crew.

Not only did the Mexicans show no mercy, but there were reports that they engaged in torture—piercing a soldier with bayonets until he died. They did not hurt the women and children, however, but did steal from their trunks and belongings. Some of the defenders were not killed immediately, but were taken prisoner.

Shortly after sunup, Santa Anna entered the Alamo as his band played a marching tune. His officers expressed surprise that there were so few rebels inside the compound because of the impressive fight they had put up. Many Mexicans had died in the fight, but Santa Anna minimized the rebels' bravery. He refused his officers' request to spare the prisoners and ordered everyone killed except for the women, children, and Joe, Travis's slave. Joe led Santa Anna to the bodies of three of the commanders: Travis, Crockett, and Bowie. Santa Anna's later report gave the men veiled praise, calling the battle scene extraordinary.

Santa Anna returned to his office, where he met with each woman separately. When he met Susanna Dickinson, he offered to adopt her daughter Angelina, but she refused. The general realized these captives would spread the news of the rebels' defeat across the region, which would serve as a lesson to anyone else with plans to revolt. He thought he would look good by releasing them. So he gave Susanna two pesos and a blanket and told her she was free to go. He then interviewed the other women, gave them money and blankets, and sent them on their way, too. The survivors left quickly, walking away from San Antonio.

Then Santa Anna ordered the removal of the bodies from the Alamo compound. The dead were separated into two groups: Loyal Mexicans were to be buried in the town cemetery, but the bodies of the rebels were to be burned. By the middle of the day, at Santa Anna's direction, soldiers had collected enough wood to start a large fire onto which they piled the bodies. More kindling was added, then more bodies. It ultimately took three piles to contain all the dead rebels. The stench was unbearable in the town, and smoke could be seen for miles.

Many of the facts of the battle were confirmed over the years by the various survivors; however, there are some things that will never be known for sure. The Battle of the Alamo has come to commemorate those who struggle and sacrifice their lives for freedom against unbelievable odds.

DEFEAT AFTER VICTORY

Other Texans were waiting around the territory for news from the Alamo. Plumes of smoke could be seen for miles, as the bodies were burned. By March 10, when no messages had come from Travis, the members at the convention for independence were worried. General Sam Houston left for San Antonio on March 11, taking 100 volunteers with him. They heard about the defeat at the Alamo when they arrived in the town of Gonzales. When the loss was confirmed to Houston, he felt responsible because he had not sent help in time to save the rebels. The settlers of Gonzales were already packing and heading east to avoid Santa Anna's army, which they expected to show up any time. Houston ordered the town of Goliad to evacuate, too.

Houston ordered James Fannin to go to Goliad, but Fannin waited several days to leave the town and then was intercepted on the plains by Mexican cavalrymen. Fannin and the Mexican troops fought, but Fannin's men were greatly outnumbered and ultimately surrendered. The Mexicans kept their prisoners in Goliad for a week, then marched 390 of them into the desert. They thought they were being taken to ships in the Gulf of Mexico for a return to the United States. Instead, they were shot or killed with swords. Twenty-eight escaped and 20 were not killed because they were doctors, mechanics, or interpreters. Two other small rebel troops were caught and killed. Santa Anna was keeping his promise to kill every American in Texas—or force them to leave. He thought now it was safe for him to head back to Mexico by ship.

THE RUNAWAY SCRAPE

As settlers tried to flee, they left almost everything they owned behind. The weather was bad; cold rain pelted the travelers. Later, this exodus was called the "Great Runaway Scrape." Houston retreated from Gonzales when he learned that the Mexican army was headed toward the town. He had the town burned as they left, along with supplies that could not be carried. The heavy cannons were sunk in the river. He had an inexperienced, poorly trained group of soldiers with him and was forced to try to train them even as they retreated. The government wanted him to stay and fight, as did many of his commanders and soldiers, but he insisted on marching away from danger.

When he and his men arrived in Harrisburg, Texas, on April 18, he learned that Santa Anna was nearby with more troops, and he led a group of men toward Lynch's Ferry on the San Jacinto River the next day. Santa Anna also was on the move. He had learned Houston was nearby and was expected to try to cross the river at Lynch's Ferry. General Martín Perfecto de Cos joined Santa Anna as Houston's men reached Lynch's Ferry a day later and took cover along the banks of the river. That afternoon, Santa Anna lined up his soldiers facing the row of trees under which Houston's men were hiding and ordered that cannons be fired on the trees, while the Mexican infantry approached under cover of this fire. Houston also had cannons, and the two sides fired at each other all day. The next morning, General Cos arrived

At San Jacinto, Santa Anna's troops were surprised by the rebels. His victory at the Alamo quickly forgotten, Santa Anna was forced to concede Texas's independence. This painting depicts the surrender of Santa Anna, shown in the uniform of a private soldier, to rebel leader Sam Houston, who convalesces under a tree.

with more than 400 men, giving the Mexicans the advantage by almost two to one.

In midafternoon on April 21, Houston received word from a scout that the Mexican camp was quiet, the men overconfident and relaxed, and many were sleeping. He quickly and quietly gave his men the order to prepare for battle, to take advantage of the unexpected opportunity. Houston's men destroyed the bridge over the river, brought the cavalry up to the flank, and moved the cannons forward. Men shouted "Remember the Alamo!" as they charged, which seemed to "increase his [the rebel soldiers'] fury during that terrible moment . . . to avenge twice over their comrades who had fallen there,"[13] according to the journal of José Enrique de la Peña, an aide to Santa Anna.

The Mexicans were totally surprised. Some were sleeping, others were doing chores, and their guns were not ready. The Mexicans did not have a chance. Some tried to run away, leaving behind about 600 of their own men killed and wounded. More than 700 were taken prisoner, and about 40 managed to escape. Santa Anna was exhausted from a day and a half spent without sleep, organizing marches and the building of barricades. He was sleeping when the Texans attacked but woke up on the first alarm and tried to run. He let his horse go, and he hid in some trees and changed into the uniform of a common soldier. Even though he waited until it was dark to cross the bayou and hide in an abandoned building, he was found and taken to Houston, who was settled on a blanket because his ankle had been broken in the fight. When presented to Houston, Santa Anna is reported to have said, "Sir, yours is no common destiny; you have captured the Napoléon of the West."[14]

Although some of his commanders urged it, Houston would not allow Santa Anna to be executed. Instead, he proposed a treaty with these terms: Santa Anna would be released and allowed to leave the territory with his troops if he would agree that Texas would be independent, with the Rio Grande as its southern border. In addition, Mexico had to return settlers' property and release prisoners.

Santa Anna returned to Mexico City after being imprisoned for seven months, only to find that he had been overthrown in his absence and was no longer president. The treaty Santa Anna had signed with Houston was not validated by the new government, but the Texans did not care. They had declared independence, fought for it, and won. The world accepted Texas as a country, and it was called the Republic of Texas, with Houston as the first president. Texas would be independent for 10 years.

Santa Anna's Later Years

The height of the revolution for Santa Anna was twofold— his success at San Antonio, followed closely by his defeat at San Jacinto. Moving upward of 6,000 soldiers more than 500 miles (805 km) with all their equipment and supplies was hard enough. But they were joined by women and children, bringing the total to 8,500. Eight hundred mules and 200 carts with oxen and assorted wagons merely complicated the entire endeavor. Many supplies were abandoned at river crossings. More than 400 died. Santa Anna was ultimately pardoned and released in part because of the intervention of American president Andrew Jackson. Santa Anna agreed to visit President Jackson in Washington, and he did this in January 1837 with a small group of faithful supporters who were all welcomed warmly. Some conjecture that Santa Anna offered to sell Texas to the United States during a private meeting with Jackson, but there is no proof that this happened, and Santa

Anna did not have the authority to make such a sale. When he finally returned to his home in Veracruz, he had been away for 14 months, and he was welcomed with parades and celebrations; the defeat at San Jacinto was apparently forgotten or at least forgiven.

Santa Anna led a quiet life for almost two years, tending to his hacienda and family and enjoying life out of the public eye. This restful time would not last, however, and he put on his uniform and returned to the battlefield in late 1838 when a French blockade of Veracruz threatened his family's safety and security. The French government had demanded payment of 600,000 pesos for damages to French property 10 years earlier. When Mexico refused to pay, the French settled in the ports of Veracruz and Tampico for more than a year, bombarding Veracruz on November 27, 1838, which escalated the standoff to a war. Santa Anna was quickly put in charge of the city's forces and prepared to defend it. When the French attacked Veracruz with a force of 3,000, a confusing battle ensued. Reports of the confrontation were as confusing as the battle, but the one made by Santa Anna—praising himself and his actions, of course—was the report most Mexicans accepted as true. This account helped return him to his former glory and enabled his election to another term as president in March 1839.

WOUNDED FOR HIS COUNTRY

During the battle with the French, Santa Anna was badly wounded in the left leg. As he wrote his reports, he believed he was dying. His written farewell to his countrymen was, as author Will Fowler says, "vintage Santa Anna." He spoke of himself as a selfless patriot in melodramatic terms and closed with the wish that his children remember him as a "good Mexican." Of course, he did not die; however, his leg had to be amputated just below the knee.

His short second stint as president (he served as acting president for only four months before Anastasio Bustamante was brought back) was marked by quite a few accomplishments.

This painting depicts an attack on the house of Santa Anna in Veracruz in 1838. After two years of retirement, Santa Anna was compelled to fight again.

He ended the war with France, paying them the money they had demanded; regulated journalists; tried to reform the constitution of 1836; and led troops against yet another revolt. He was happy to return to the relative calm of his haciendas and his children once again. However, in late 1840, Bustamante had lost some of his prime supporters over a variety of issues, and several different groups invited Santa Anna to return to politics. In late summer of 1841, he began a letter-writing campaign encouraging Bustamante to listen to the people who were tired of his government. Santa Anna offered himself as mediator between Bustamante and the rebels, but he

WEAPONS OF WAR

The weapons used to defend the Alamo were as varied as the defending soldiers. Although some Texians were issued guns taken from the Mexicans who had surrendered with General Martín Perfecto de Cos after the Battle of Bexar the previous December, most of these volunteers were not issued firearms. Rather they brought with them the weapons they carried as part of their daily lives.

Common guns were the Pennsylvania/Kentucky rifle, the double-barreled shotgun, the long rifle, and flintlock gun. The troops who came from New Orleans may have carried the U.S. Common Rifle of 1817, which was issued by the military. Many of the defenders probably had trade rifles, which were practical because they were inexpensive and less delicate than the long rifle.

Mexican soldiers often carried surplus weapons from their war for independence from Spain. After the mid-1820s, most of Mexico's regular soldiers carried regulation guns bought from England. The goal was to have a standard for weapons to make supply of ammunition and repairs easier.

One of the most common weapons was the India Pattern musket, or "Brown Bess," that weighed more than 9 pounds was ignored. In mid-September, he headed for Mexico City, where he prepared to return the government to a position of strength. Battles broke out on the streets of the city, and finally, on October 5, Bustamante agreed to end the fighting and to be replaced by Santa Anna as president.

SUCCESS IN POLITICS

After a series of presidents whose terms had been brief, the Mexican people were ready for someone who would hold on to office for the full term, and they put their faith in Santa Anna. He began his longest term as president in October 1841.

(4 kg) and came with a 17-inch (43.18 cm) bayonet that brought the weight up another pound. These guns were not easy to use. Each shot required the soldier to load powder, tamp it, and then load the ball shot. According to the University of Texas A&M Web site, the powder the Mexicans used was of low quality. They had to load cartridges with so much powder that the inside of the barrel often became clogged, and they had to use a smaller ball to compensate. The Brown Bess was very accurate at close range—less than 70 yards (64 m), for example—which describes most of the fighting at the Alamo.

The Baker rifle was a well-made weapon the Mexicans also bought from the British. Some rifles came with a 23-inch (58.42 cm) bayonet and weighed close to 9 pounds (4 kg). The Baker was relatively short, with a 30-inch (76.2 cm) barrel, but had good sights, enabling more accurate shots. The bayonet was unwieldy, though, and sometimes simply fell off after a few shots.

The Tower flintlock carbine of 1812 was an English musket the Mexicans used until the 1850s. The blunderbuss was another weapon, coming in several forms, which may have been carried by some of the Tejano defenders and Mexican attackers. The blunderbuss was short, with a flared muzzle.

For the bulk of the first two years in office, he governed virtually alone while the new Congress was formed. The new constitution, ratified in 1843, stipulated that he be elected again, and this election took place at the end of the summer of 1843, putting him back into office.

Santa Anna ensured that the legislature was well stocked with Santanistas who agreed with his traditional, liberal, and centrist viewpoints, ushering in a period of stability. Many of the men in key positions were Veracruzanos. His goals were simple and straightforward. He wanted to provide peace, prosperity, and a continuation of the nation's traditions and customs, while guaranteeing people's rights, fair elections, and ample educational opportunities. The government maintained three separate branches—executive, legislative, and judicial— but gave the president enough power to exert influence if necessary.

He was a popular president, dedicated to improving the lives of the poor, bringing education to the masses, and donating land to the homeless. He also strengthened the army and improved the privileges accorded to those who served in the military. Santa Anna recognized the importance of a strong military presence as the United States began to exert more power. He instituted many reforms, including improvements to roads, the port of Veracruz, and the main marketplace in Mexico City; and better relations with other countries. His government supported the Roman Catholic Church as the official religion of Mexico; however, he also taxed the church to help pay for military improvements. Taxes were increased for everyone in the country and were one of the elements that led to discontent with his government and its eventual downfall. Increasingly, it was said that these taxes were used to pay for the large haciendas owned by Santa Anna and many of his friends and supporters. At this time, it was possible to find statues of the general, buildings and streets named after him, and festivals held in his honor. Many of these buildings, structures, and events were

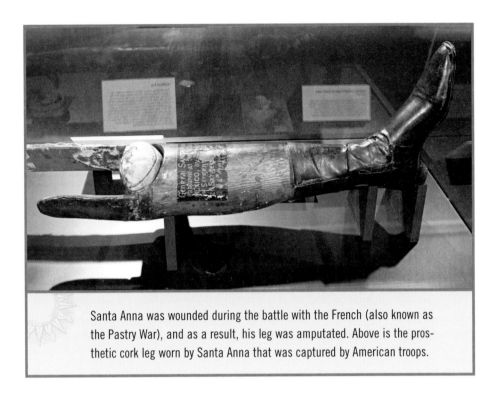

Santa Anna was wounded during the battle with the French (also known as the Pastry War), and as a result, his leg was amputated. Above is the prosthetic cork leg worn by Santa Anna that was captured by American troops.

orchestrated by Santa Anna himself, in his constant need for attention and approval.

TROUBLES

Another issue in this administration was Santa Anna's insistence on reconquering Texas, which was now an independent entity, recognized as such by most of the rest of the world. The British consul who visited Mexico City in an attempt to change the president's mind about Texas sent a dismal report back to London. Queen Victoria's representative, Pakenham, tried to convince Santa Anna that recognition of Texas would create a buffer between Mexico and the United States. He warned that attempts to reclaim the province might lead Texas to join America. But none of Pakenham's arguments did any good. In fact, Santa Anna's army had been waging battles in Texas almost since the day he took office in 1841. It took him three years to come to the understanding that he was not going to be able to reclaim the territory for Mexico, and only then did he recognize its independence.

Meanwhile, his personal life was in turmoil. His wife died on August 23, 1844, after being sick on and off for two years. A day of prayer was observed along with a formal grand funeral and public mourning. Santa Anna wasted no time in remarrying. On October 3, he married the 15-year-old daughter of a very rich businessman. Dolores Tosta was sent to meet her husband, who was 35 years older than her, after he once again married in absentia. Dolores was almost the same age as her stepchildren, but she must have been quite mature for her years. She refused to live in the hacienda because she did not like country living. Instead, she insisted that Santa Anna buy her a house in Mexico City, where she spent most of her time until her death in 1886. Dolores became known as *La flor de Mexico,* or "The flower of Mexico," and she lived the life of a rich woman. She was showered with jewelry and gifts by her husband, and she threw and also attended many parties in the capital city. The couple had no children. Even though they did not spend much time together, during critical times in his older years Santa Anna was able to rely on Dolores for moral and emotional support.

At the end of November 1844, a coup attempt against Santa Anna's government was led by General Mariano Paredes y Arrillaga in Guadalajara. What Santa Anna took to be an insignificant and isolated incident was really a sign of deeper breakdown in his popularity. Suddenly, his excessive taxation and spending were intolerable. Three of his closest advisers had resigned the month before, including Tornel, his friend of 30 years, and he had no one he could trust. In Mexico City, one of his statues was knocked down, and others were defaced. He declared that he was still the president, and he threatened to march his troops into the city to prove it. Santa Anna quickly realized, however, that he did not have the manpower to carry out these threats, and he wrote to the new government on January 10, 1845, telling them he had renounced the presidency and intended to leave the country. As he attempted to return to his hacienda outside Xalapa, he was captured and humiliated with imprisonment in his own hometown.

EXILE AND TRIUMPHANT RETURN

Santa Anna was officially charged with attacking the country's legitimate political system under the constitution of 1843 and with other offenses. He spent five months in jail but was never tried. He agreed to leave Mexico, and the charges were dropped. Santa Anna, Dolores, and his seven-year old son, Manuel, sailed to Cuba, where they were greeted warmly by the Spanish commander of the island. The family spent 14 months in Havana, returning to Veracruz on August 16, 1846. Once again, Santa Anna returned to a position of authority and power, seemingly having worked magic to enable Mexicans to forget in such a short period of time all the hatred that they had felt toward him at the end of his last term as president.

> The most illustrious of its children is home again; he who has saved us always during the great conflicts. . . . The courageous and great Santa Anna is in Veracruz. God has saved Mexico.
> —From a pamphlet at the time of his return, August 1846[15]

Not everyone believed he had returned to help the country; many were sure he was back only to help himself. Within two months, he was elected president once again. And just like the elections of 1833, Gómez Farías was elected vice president. Santa Anna stayed away from Mexico City, preferring to organize troops to face off against the United States should the unrest come to outright warfare. Farías was left in charge with the job of raising money to support Santa Anna's expedition. This last responsibility was never met, and Santa Anna ended up financing much of what the troops required, including food, weapons, ammunition, and uniforms.

MEXICAN-AMERICAN WAR

A major battle of the Mexican-American War took place on February 22–23, 1847, with Santa Anna attacking American forces led by Zachary Taylor. The Americans had the advantage of position, located in uneven terrain behind natural outcroppings and within a gully that narrowed at one end. Although the Mexicans outnumbered the Americans, the Battle of Angostura–Buena Vista did not have a clear outcome.

The capture of Veracruz by American general Winfield Scott on March 28 was a low point for Santa Anna. He felt sorrow for the port city and shame as the country's leader. But he immediately headed for Xalapa, where he gathered his army once again and prepared to fend off Scott's advance inland at high ground known as Cerro Gordo, or "Fat Hill." The attack was well planned and brutal. Thousands of Mexicans died, and Santa Anna was forced to retreat, as Scott's army was able to move farther into the country. Santa Anna was tired and defeated. He offered to resign on May 18 but was encouraged by some of his old colleagues to rescind his resignation. He returned to Mexico City, where he planned to organize another army. Scott was not far from the capital and realistically could have taken it without much trouble.

At this point, Santa Anna became something of a double agent. He entered into secret negotiations with the U.S. government, using Englishmen as emissaries. He agreed to talk the Mexican Congress into accepting Scott's terms for surrender for a certain amount of money; however, he had no intention of doing any such thing. Instead, he earned a substantial sum while the Americans wasted time waiting for talks that would never materialize. None of this trickery would help Santa Anna, however, as the Americans and Mexicans fought hard only a few miles outside Mexico City. An armistice, or truce, was called, though each side claimed the other had asked for the truce to discuss peace terms. And although a treaty was proposed, fighting resumed on September 6, and Mexico City was overrun. The American flag flew over the Mexican National

The American army occupies Mexico City during the Mexican-American War, in this nineteenth-century American painting. The defeat left Santa Anna with a dwindling supply of soldiers, and he was soon relieved of his command.

Palace, and yet Santa Anna did not see this defeat as the end of the war. The Mexican government went to Querétaro, and Santa Anna also left, with his army, to reorganize.

No attempts at reorganization, however, would be enough to keep the Mexican soldiers from deserting en masse. Within days, Santa Anna had lost 500 men, and within two weeks, the army had shrunk to one-fourth its original size. While he was trying to figure out what to do, and making small incursions against some American outposts, the government relieved him of command. Accusations appeared in newspapers calling him a traitor, and others accused him of trying to thwart the peace agreement the Mexican government was about to sign with the United States.

The Treaty of Guadalupe Hidalgo was signed on February 2, 1848, and gave almost half the country's territories north of the Rio Grande to the United States, which in turn paid Mexico $15 million.

EXILED AGAIN, AND HOME AGAIN

Santa Anna and his family left the country several weeks later and spent two years in Jamaica and three years in Colombia. During his absence, he became one of the generals who was investigated and blamed for the tragic loss of so much Mexican land. Congressman Ramón Gamboa, who had first accused Santa Anna of treason in 1847, repeated that accusation and added a long list of reasons for his charges. His statement was supported by Carlos María de Bustamante. Historians see the Mexican land loss as occurring through a series of mistakes and lopsided situations and events that could not have been carried out by one man.

Unbelievably, Santa Anna was not finished yet as a leader of his country. He returned to Veracruz on April 1, 1853, inspired and encouraged by some of his former Santanistas, led by Tornel, who was friendly again with the exiled former president. Once again, the Mexican people welcomed Santa Anna home with open arms and fiestas. But he faced a chaotic atmosphere and many challenges as he was asked to help the country find peace and restore the constitution. He was installed as a temporary dictator, with the arrangement that he would be allowed to retire to his hacienda once certain goals were reached. Although the dictatorship was intended to be short-lived, it stretched to August 1855 and became increasingly repressive: Many former leaders were exiled; the press was censored; secret police spied on the people; and anyone considered to be subversive was tried and executed if found guilty. Individual municipal and state governments were closed, and a strong national army was once again built, using increased taxes and borrowed money. Santa Anna was given the title *Alteza Serenísma,* or "Serene Highness." He had come to believe that the only way for Mexico to survive and prosper was to be united under one political system; there was no room for the different factions to thrive, since their existence had given rise to the revolts and coups of the past.

Certain positive changes were made during his dictatorship, including the building of new lines of communication such as telegraph lines, improvements to roads, installation of gas street lamps in Mexico City, and upgrades to the city's water system. He also focused his attention on improving education, judicial reform, and the country's infrastructure.

THE PRESIDENT'S LAST STAND

But, as always, it was not to last long. After three of his advisers died in the summer of 1853, he seemed to lack focus and grew increasingly repressive and controlling. After a successful revolt by his enemies, he abdicated on August 12, 1855. He and family members promptly went into exile for a third time. This time there would be no revival or triumphant return. He was remembered only as a traitor, tyrant, and opportunist. Mexico was to change dramatically during the 20 years Santa Anna spent in exile. The men he had fought with in his early career were dead or very old. The military men and politicians moving up in the ranks did not remember the War of Independence and did not understand why Santa Anna had been so revered. Mexico entered a new era characterized by reforms in government, the Catholic Church, and the military.

LAST EXILE

Santa Anna spent the years away from Mexico in Colombia, St. Thomas, New Jersey, and New York. He dabbled in Mexican politics from afar, attempting to manipulate his way back into favor. He encouraged the country to adopt a constitutional

SANTA ANNA'S MIXED LEGACY

Much has been written about the battle of the Alamo from the viewpoint of its defenders and their supporters and by American historians and writers. An intriguing and detailed account of the Texas Revolution, the assault on the Alamo, and personal insights into Santa Anna's methods are found in the book *With Santa Anna in Texas* by Lieutenant José Enrique de la Peña, an officer on Santa Anna's staff.

One of the most interesting questions he raises is about the final assault on the Alamo. Why did Santa Anna insist on attacking when he knew that William Travis planned either to surrender or escape the next day? De la Peña suggests that Santa Anna needed a bloody ending for Mexico to seem more glorious. Perhaps that is also why Santa Anna insisted on killing the seven surviving American soldiers. His officers saw this as outright murder, unjustified by any acts of the enemy.

De la Peña's journal is fascinating in some of its details of the trek into Texas. He claims that preparations were not well made and that medical care was lacking—not only for those who would be wounded in battle but also for those who would succumb to typical campaign illnesses. He writes that Santa Anna did not adequately scout out the terrain beforehand. Rivers were not measured, adequate protection was not provided for weapons and ammunition, and overall planning was lacking. He also blames Santa Anna for impressing, or forcing the involvement of, ordinary citizens such as craftsmen, businessmen, farmers, and even criminals. These "soldiers" were fighting men in name only.

monarchy and even suggested Austrian archduke Ferdinand Maximilian for the position. He did return to Veracruz on February 27, 1864, expecting the customary adulations as he disembarked. Before he left the ship, he was asked to sign a document that was written in French, which he did not understand. He was told he was pledging allegiance to the new government, but he was not told it also said he must abstain from any political intervention, written or verbal. By

Interestingly, de la Peña made the observation that the troops should have been transported north by ship across the Gulf of Mexico, which would have served the double purpose of cutting off the enemy's supplies, which came in by ship, and would also have been faster, resulting in fewer casualties.

De la Peña writes that Santa Anna pursued the attack against the rebels in Texas mainly for personal reasons. He claims that Santa Anna appointed himself commander in chief of the operation and, instead of preparing for the battle secretly and carefully, was publicly boastful. He claims that Santa Anna's "interests were in war, for war would increase his fame, that chimera which so attracts the human heart, especially a soldier's heart." Santa Anna also was accused in newspaper articles of "pursuing ambitious ends,"[16] with some editors accusing him of promoting war. And lastly, de la Peña belittles Santa Anna's claim that he was the Napoléon of the West. He characterizes those who agreed as merely trying to flatter their leader. He agrees that Santa Anna's character was similar to Napoléon's, but that he lacked the "daring and enterprising genius"[17] of Napoléon. He also claims Santa Anna did not have the knowledge of science, history, or language and did not possess the qualities of personality found in great leaders—the ability to inspire and command an army, and a mind that would be superior to that of the enemy. "Resources (financial) were not lacking; what was lacking was prudence, planning, order, foresight, clear and precise judgment . . . and more capital than was necessary has been invested in this disastrous expedition."[18]

publishing a manifesto the day he arrived, he broke that pledge and was ordered out of Mexico once again. This somewhat underhanded method of ensuring Santa Anna did not remain in Mexico was done out of fear that he would somehow stage another miraculous comeback, ruining the government that had been carefully implemented during the nine years of his exile. He quickly recanted his support of the monarchy and continued to make public statements against the empire.

TRAITOR?

Santa Anna's enemies characterized him as an imperialist out to ruin his country, and he defended himself the best he could against claims of treason. He proclaimed his innocence and declared himself a loyal Mexican, who only, as always, wanted the best for his country and his people. That fervent desire sometimes led him to make rash decisions and mistakes. However, he was rejected by his countrymen and labeled a charlatan. His career goals and dedication were misunderstood by this new generation of Mexican liberals. Santa Anna claimed he was a man who was a patriot above all else, a "good Mexican." But he had actually betrayed every interest he had ever stood for.

Finally, on September 2, 1867, having been imprisoned in San Juan de Ulúa, Santa Anna was formally charged with treason and tried in Veracruz. The charges against him included: inviting a European prince to take over Mexico's government and offering to participate in that government; signing a document recognizing the empire and promising not to speak or write publicly on its behalf (1864); and becoming involved in the conflict of 1867, after he was forbidden to do so. The prosecution requested the death penalty under the Law of 1862.

He defended himself by saying he did not remember signing any documents in support of a constitutional monarchy; he had not taken advantage of opportunities to install a monarchy in the past; and that he could not be charged under a law that was passed eight years after the crime he had allegedly committed. The court-martial board agreed with many of Santa Anna's arguments, and rather than facing a firing squad, he once again faced exile. He was sentenced to eight years for treason.

So, at 73 years of age and in frail health, the founder of the Mexican Republic was forced to leave the land he loved with the stain of "traitor" on his name and forever tarnishing his reputation.

This time, Dolores remained behind in Mexico City. Santa Anna spent the next seven years living in Havana, Puerto Plata, and Nassau, writing and attempting to restore some honor to his name. He was allowed to return to Mexico, which he did on February 27, 1874. Santa Anna was 80 years old and partially blind. No one recognized him except his family, who met him in Orizaba. Dolores cared for Santa Anna in her home in Mexico City until his death at age 82 in 1876.

CONCLUSION

Born into a middle-class family in the Mexican state of Veracruz toward the end of the eighteenth century, Antonio de Padua María Severino López de Santa Anna y Pérez de Lebrón was an experienced military leader who won many awards and was revered by his people. He owned vast tracts of land in his home province, where he entertained the top dignitaries of the day. He built up communities, running them with a careful hand. Education, legal reform, military strength, infrastructure repair, and national pride and honor were close to his heart, and in his six terms as president of the republic,

SANTA ANNA'S OBITUARY, PUBLISHED IN *EL SIGLO XIX*

General Santa Anna—The last hours of his life inspire the saddest of reflections: the man who controlled millions, who acquired fortunes and honors, who exercised an unrestricted dictatorship, has died in the midst of the greatest want, abandoned by all except a few of his friends who remembered him in adversity. A relic of another epoch, our generation remembered him for the misfortunes he brought upon the republic, forgetting the really eminent services he rendered to the nation. He was as a tree, stricken in years, destitute of foliage, to whose boughs even such parasites as are usually found on dry and withered trees did not cling.

he instituted many laws that would improve the lives of his fellow Mexicans.

He was smart but impulsive, with a quick temper and arrogant tendencies. He could be ruthless and manipulative. He was a hard worker and energetic, yet sometimes turned those energies to less-than-positive pursuits. He gambled away a fortune and fathered several children out of wedlock, but was a devoted father to them all. He pushed his men hard in the field, but he pushed himself just as hard. He was ambitious and did not hesitate to break the rules to get his way. He was loved and hated, respected and feared. He lived a long life and watched his beloved Mexico move from a Spanish territory to an independent republic, able to govern itself. He saw the country lose half its land in a deal with the United States, and he lived through three exiles and three triumphant returns before he died a broken, penniless man, forgotten for his accomplishments and remembered only as a traitor.

Santa Anna was the Hero of Tampico, Liberator of Veracruz, Founder of the Republic, and a warrior who gave a leg for his country's independence. He was shrewd and perceptive, with a way of appearing on the scene at just the right moment, when public opinion had turned against the man in power. He had a knack for public relations and wrote and printed up pamphlets, speeches, and newspaper articles, all raising him to the status of myth. He was inspirational and had boundless energy. He was bright and charismatic, and people wanted to like him. They wanted to believe he was what he proclaimed to be. He was like a phoenix, rising from the ashes of defeat to rule again and again.

Chronology

1794   **February 21** Antonio de Padua María Severino López de Santa Anna is born in Xalapa in the state of Veracruz, Mexico.

1810   Santa Anna joins the Mexican army although he is underage.

        September 16 The War of Independence begins.

1811   **April** Santa Anna's first experience in battle in Aguayo. He is promoted to lieutenant.

1813   Santa Anna has his first run-in with his superiors when he is disciplined for forging signatures in order to get money to pay his gambling debts.

        November 6 Mexico declares itself independent from Spain.

1816–1817   Santa Anna serves as aide to Governor José García Dávila.

        December 29, 1816 Santa Anna is promoted to captain.

1819–1821   Santa Anna is charged with establishing and reestablishing several municipalities in which insurgent soldiers and their families will live.

1821   **February 24** The Plan of Iguala is drawn up by insurgent Vicente Guerrero and royalist commander Agustín de Iturbide. Santa Anna switches sides and is promoted to lieutenant colonel. Santa Anna plays instrumental roles in several major battles.

1822   Santa Anna is promoted to colonel and appointed commander of Xalapa. In the fall, he is named commander of the entire province of Veracruz. In October, he is promoted to brigadier general and calls for Mexico to become a republic.

1824   A new constitution is adopted. Guadalupe Victoria is president.

1825   Santa Anna and María Inés de la Paz García are married. He buys his hacienda, Manga de Clavo, where the couple lives privately for two years.

1826 Santa Anna emerges from retirement to put down a revolt. He is appointed vice governor of Veracruz in September.

1829 He again goes into retirement at Manga de Clavo, until 1832.

1833 Santa Anna becomes president; however, he leaves Vice President Valentín Gómez Farías in charge as he once again retreats to his hacienda.

1835 Santa Anna goes to Mexico City to serve his term as president until 1836, when he leaves his new vice president in charge. Miguel Barragán is acting president. A new constitution replaces the one of 1824. The Texas revolt begins.

1836 The Battle of the Alamo takes place on March 6, followed by the Battle of San Jacinto on April 22. Santa Anna is taken prisoner and spends seven months in

1822
Santa Anna is promoted to brigadier general and calls for Mexico to become a republic

1794
Antonio de Padua María Severino López de Santa Anna is born in Xalapa in the state of Veracruz, Mexico

1826
Santa Anna emerges from retirement to put down a revolt

1833
Santa Anna becomes president

1794

1836

1810
Santa Anna joins the Mexican army although he is underage; the War of Independence begins

1825
Santa Anna and María Inés de la Paz García are married

1836
The Battle of the Alamo takes place on March 6, followed by the Battle of San Jacinto on April 22

jail. He is released, and the 1836 constitution is put into place.

1837   Santa Anna visits U.S. president Andrew Jackson in Washington and then returns to Manga de Clavo.

1838   Santa Anna is wounded and loses his leg in the Battle of Veracruz.

1841–1844   Santa Anna is president. His wife dies in August 1844, and he marries his second wife, Dolores Tosta, in October.

1845   Santa Anna is exiled to Cuba after being overthrown in December 1844.

1846   He returns to Mexico and mobilizes an army to march against U.S. general Zachary Taylor, whose troops are marching south into Mexico.

1838
Santa Anna is wounded and loses his leg in the Battle of Veracruz

1847
Santa Anna's army is defeated by Scott at the Battle of Cerro Gordo

1867
Santa Anna is arrested in July and court-martialed. Exiled for eight years and lives in Havana, Puerto Plata, and Nassau

1876
Santa Anna dies

1838   1876

1858
The Mexican Civil War begins and lasts until 1860

1841–1844
Santa Anna is president. His wife dies in August 1844, and he marries his second wife, Dolores Tosta, in October

1874
Santa Anna is allowed to return to Mexico on February 27. He is 80 years old

1847 U.S. general Winfield Scott overtakes Veracruz in March and Santa Anna retreats to Mexico City. On April 18, Santa Anna's army is defeated by Scott at the Battle of Cerro Gordo. On September 15, Mexico City falls to the American army.

1848 The Treaty of Guadalupe Hidalgo gives half of Mexico's lands to the United States. In March, Santa Anna goes into exile in Jamaica and then in Colombia.

1853 Santa Anna returns from exile and becomes dictator.

1854 Santa Anna goes into exile again in Colombia and then St. Thomas.

1855 Santa Anna abdicates and goes into exile.

1858 The Mexican Civil War begins and lasts until 1860.

1862 British, French, and Spanish troops attack Veracruz. Mexico City falls to the French, and Austrian archduke Ferdinand Maximilian is installed as head of Mexico.

1863 Maximilian orders Santa Anna to leave Mexico, and he returns to St. Thomas.

1864 Santa Anna arrives in Veracruz, planning to liberate the city. He is not allowed to disembark and signs a document in French promising not to try to incite rebellion.

1866 Santa Anna is tricked into believing that the United States will help him retake power in Mexico.

1867 Santa Anna is arrested in July and court-martialed. He is exiled for eight years and lives in Havana, Puerto Plata, and Nassau.

1874 Santa Anna is allowed to return to Mexico on February 27. He is 80 years old.

1876 Santa Anna dies.

Notes

Chapter 2

1 Calderón de la Barca, *Life in Mexico*. Boston: Little, Brown, 1843, p. 37.
2 Will Fowler, *Santa Anna of Mexico*. Lincoln: University of Nebraska Press, 2007, p. 19.

Chapter 3

3 Donald E. Chipman, *Southwestern Historical Quarterly* XCI, no. 2 (October 1987): 128. The Texas State Historical Association, with the Center for Studies in Texas History, University of Texas at Austin.
4. "Who Were the 'Coahuiltecans'?" Texas Beyond History. http://www.texasbeyond history.net.
5 Morris Bishop, *The Odyssey of Cabeza de Vaca*. Westport, Conn.: Greenwood Press Publishers. 1933, 1971, p. 98.

Chapter 4

6 Fowler, *Santa Anna of Mexico*. 2007, p. 29.
7 Ibid., p. 34.

Chapter 5

8 Ibid., p. 117.
9 Ibid., p. 139.

Chapter 6

10 Ibid., p. 150.
11 Ibid., p. 154.

Chapter 7

12 Timothy M. Matovina, *The Alamo Remembered: Tejano Accounts and Perspectives*. Austin: University of Texas Press, 1995, pp. 84–85.
13 Carmen Perry, trans. and ed., *With Santa Anna in Texas: A Personal Narrative of the Revolution by José Enrique de la Peña*. College Station: Texas A&M University Press, 1975, p. 131.
14 Wallace L. McKeehan. "Antonio López de Santa Anna." Texas A&M University. http://www. tamu.edu/ccbn/dewitt/ santaanna.htm.

Chapter 8

15 Fowler, *Santa Anna of Mexico*. p. 256.
16 Perry, *With Santa Anna in Texas*. p. 10.
17 Ibid., p. 11.
18 Ibid., p. 7.

Bibliography

de la Barca, Calderón. *Life in Mexico.* Boston: Little, Brown, 1843.

Bishop, Morris. *The Odyssey of Cabeza de Vaca.* Westport, Conn.: Greenwood Press Publishers, 1933, 1971.

Chipman, Donald E. *Southwestern Historical Quarterly* XCI, no. 2 (October 1987). The Texas State Historical Association, with the Center for Studies in Texas History, University of Texas at Austin.

Fowler, Will. *Santa Anna of Mexico.* Lincoln: University of Nebraska Press, 2007.

Levy, Janey. *The Alamo: A Primary Source History of the Legendary Texas Mission.* New York: Rosen Publishing Group, 2003.

Matovina, Timothy M. *The Alamo Remembered: Tejano Accounts and Perspectives.* Austin: University of Texas Press, 1995.

Murphy, Jim. *Inside the Alamo.* New York: Delacort Press, 2003.

Perry, Carmen, trans. and ed. *With Santa Anna in Texas: A Personal Narrative of the Revolution by José Enrique de la Peña.* College Station: Texas A&M University Press, 1975.

Tanaka, Shelley. *A Day That Changed America: The Alamo.* New York: Hyperion, 2003.

Warrick, Karen Clemens. *Alamo: Victory or Death on the Texas Frontier.* Berkeley Heights, N.J.: Enslow Publishers, 2009.

Web Sites

www.americanhistory.suite101.com

www.britannica.com

www.tamu.edu

www.texasbeyondhistory.net

Further Reading

Castañeda, Carlos E. *The Mexican Side of the Texas Revolution (1836) by the Chief Mexican Participants*. Austin, Tex.: Graphic Ideas, 1970.

Crawford, Ann Fears, ed. *The Eagle: The Autobiography of Santa Anna*. Austin, Tex.: State House Press, 1988.

Hardin, Stephen L. *The Alamo 1836: Santa Anna's Texas Campaign*. London: Osprey Publishing, 2001.

Long, Jeff. *Duel of Eagles: The Mexican and U.S. Fight for the Alamo*. New York: William Morrow and Co., 1990.

Picture Credits

Index

1832 Civil War
  events of 45–47

A

Aguayo 30
Alamo
  aftermath 67–70
  arrival in 58–60
  attack on 6, 18, 27,
    54–67, 84
  defenders of 7–8, 18,
    27, 54–67, 74, 84
  paintings of 34
  remember the 6–8, 69
  road to 51–54
  women and children at
    6, 8, 54–55, 60, 65–66
Almonte, Juan 58, 63
Álvarez de Pineda,
  Alonso 19
Amoladeras 30
Angostura-Buena Vista,
  Battle of 80
Apache tribe 18–19, 23
Apodaca, Juan Ruiz
  de 32
Archer, Christon 33
Arista, Mariano 49
Arizona 20
Arkansas 25
Army of the People
  left for San Antonio
    53–54
Arredondo y Mioño,
  Joaquín de 30–31
Asís, Francisco de 32
Atakapa tribe 23
Austin, Moses 25, 51
Austin, Stephen 25,
  47–48
  jailed 52
  and Texas
    independence 51–53
Avavares tribe 22
Aztec Indian settlement
  11, 20

B

Baker rifle 75
Banco de Avío 45

Barca, Frances Erskine
  Calderón de la
  Life in Mexico 12, 14
Barradas, Isidro 44
Barragán, Miguel 50
Belize 20
Bonham, Jim
  and the Alamo 55
Bourbon family 37
Bowie, James
  and the Alamo 34, 55,
    58–61, 66
  and Texas
    independence 53
Brazos River 51
Broadsides
  Santa Anna on 15
Brown Bess 75
Bustamante, Anastasio
  government 44–46,
    73–75
Bustamante, Carlos
  María de

C

Cabeza de Vaca, Álvar
  Núñez 21–25
Caddo tribe 18–19
Calderón, José María
  45–46
California
  settlements 20
Canada 25–26
Caribbean Sea 20
Catholicism 51
  in Mexico 16, 19, 34,
    39–40, 47, 50, 76, 83
  missionaries 25
Cerro Gordo 80
childhood 9–17
cholera epidemics 49
Cincunegui, Ignacio
  32
Ciudad Victoria 30
Coahuila 58
Coahuiltecan tribe 18
Cofre de Perote
  mountain 12
Colorado
  settlements 20, 25

Columbia
  exile in 82–83
Comanche tribe 18–19
community builder
  32–33
Córdoba 37
Cortés, Hernán 11,
  19–21
Cos, José 16
Cos, Martín Perfecto de
  and the Mexican army
    52–54, 56, 68, 74
criollo class 16, 41
Crockett, Davy
  and the Alamo 8, 34,
    65–66
Cuba 44
  exile in 79, 87
Culiacán 23

D

Dávila, José García
  government 31, 33, 36
Dawn at the Alamo
  (painting) 34, 57
death 87
Dickinson, Almeron 54
Dickinson, Angelina
  54, 66
Dickinson, Susanna 54,
  66
dictator
  temporary 82–83
Dorantes, Andres de
  Carranza 24–25

E

education 9
El Libertador. *See*
  Iturbide, Agustín de
  (El Libertador)
Encero, El hacienda 9, 46
Esparza, Ana 54
Esparza, Enrique 65
Estevanico 25
exile 79, 82–85

F

family
  connections 32, 36

middle-class 9–10,
    17, 87
Fannin, Jim
    and the Alamo 55, 61
    and Texas
    independence 53,
    67
Farías, Gómez 79
Farías, Valentín Gómez
    47, 52
Fixed Infantry Regiment
    of Veracruz 29
Florida
    settlements 19, 21
Fowler, Will 46, 72
France
    explorers 25
    government 25, 72
    military 72, 74
    missionaries 19, 25
    occupation of Mexico
    15

G
Galveston Island 21
Gamboa, Ramón 82
García, María Inéz de la
    Paz (wife) 41–42
    death 78
Goliad 24, 55, 59–61, 67
Gonzales 52, 55, 59–60,
    67–68
Gonzales, Petra 54
Great Britain 77
Guadalajara 78
Guadalupe Victoria 40,
    42
Guanajuato 49
Guatemala 20
Guerrero, Vincente 34,
    42, 45
Gulf of Mexico 12, 20,
    23, 68, 85

H
Harrisburg, Texas 68
Houston 51
Houston, Samuel
    after the Alamo 67–70

and the Alamo 57, 60
    Texas' first president 70

I
illnesses
    amputation 72
    wounds 72–75
Indians
    battles against 9
Iturbide, Agustín de
    (El Libertador) 34,
    36–38
Iturrigarary, Viceroy José
    de 11

J
Jackson, Andrew 71
Jalisco 44
Jamaica 19
    exile in 82

K
Karankawa tribe 18–19,
    21–22

L
La Salle, Robert de 25
later years 71–88
Lebrón, Manuela Pérez
    (mother) 10
    death 31
    and politics 16
legacy
    mixed 84–85
    traitor 86–87
Levy, Janey 34
Life in Mexico (Barca)
    12, 14
Liñán, Pascual 32
Loma de Santa María
    32
Louisiana 25
Louisiana Purchase 25
Lynch's Ferry 68

M
Maldonado, Alonso
    Castillo 25
Malhado island 21

Manga de Clavo haci-
    enda 9, 40–41, 44, 50
Mariame tribe 22
Maximilian, Ferinan 84
Maya Indians 56
McArdle, Henry Arthur
    34, 57
Medellín 32
Medina, Battle of
    30–31
Medina River 58
Mestizo 41
Mexican-American War
    events of 80–82
Mexican War of
    Independence 10, 14
    events of 28, 36, 40,
    74, 83
Mexico
    army 6–8, 31, 34, 40–
    41, 44, 47, 51, 54–70,
    74–76, 78–81, 83–85
    constitution 20, 38–40,
    46, 50, 76, 79, 82–83,
    86
    economy 20, 45
    fights for independence
    9, 14, 16, 27, 29,
    34–35, 74, 86
    government 12, 20,
    31–33, 38–40, 43–47,
    49–52, 58, 70, 72,
    74–86
    history of 18–27
    independence 14–15,
    17, 20, 25, 34, 37, 44,
    49, 88
    laws 52, 88
    loss of land 82
    new republic 39–50
    people 20, 40–41, 49,
    75–76, 79, 82, 84,
    86–88
    politics 20, 49
    rebellions 11, 20, 27,
    29–33, 38, 40, 42,
    44–50, 74–75, 83
    reforms 20, 42, 47, 50,
    74, 76, 83, 87

secret police 82
taxes 36, 47, 76, 83
trade 15
Mexico City 11, 37
  capital 20, 31–32,
    40–41, 45, 47–50, 61,
    75–80, 83, 87
  capture of 80–81
  living in 9, 16, 78
  railroad in 12
  return to 70, 87
military
  battles 18, 24, 27–28,
    30–31, 51–70, 77, 80
  capture 70–71
  commander general 36
  colonel 28
  commander 11, 42–43,
    56, 81, 85
  early career 10, 16–17,
    28–38
  financial backers 11,
    15, 45, 56, 79, 85
  finding his calling
    15–17
  General 34, 37–38, 54,
    76, 87–88
  heroism 17, 49
  lieutenant 30
  lieutenant colonel 33
  medals 30
  troops 14–15, 18, 30–
    31, 36–37, 45–47, 49,
    51–52, 54–69, 71–72,
    74, 77–81, 83–85
Misión San Antonio de
  Valero 27
Monterrey 24

N
Napoléon Bonaparte 56
Narváez, Pánfilo de 21,
  23
Nassau
  exile in 87
Nevada 20
New Jersey
  exile in 83
New Mexico 20

New York
  exile in 83

O
O'Donojú, Juan 37
Orizaba 12, 37, 46, 87

P
Pacific Ocean 20
Pakenham 77
Pánuco River 21
Paredesy Arrillaga,
  Mariano 78
Pedrazza, Manuel
  Gómez 44, 46–47
Peña, José Enrique de
  la 70
  With Santa Anna in
    Texas 84–85
personal life 41–42
  back to the hacienda
    44–45
  marriage 40–42, 78
personality
  determination 30, 32,
    88
  joker 30
  ladies' man 30
  risk taker 32, 88
  ruthlessness 30, 33, 88
Pico de Orizaba volcano
  12
Plan of Casa Mata 38
Plan of Cuernavaca
  49–50
Plan of Iguala 34–35
politics
  back to power 11,
    74–76, 79
  career 42–46, 75–77
  offices 11, 33, 40,
    42–43, 47–49, 83
  troubles 77–79
Ponce de León 19
populist leader 36–37
porteño 10
presidency 87
  coup attempts 70, 78
  during the Texas war

for independence 52,
  54, 56, 61
first term 39, 47–50
fourth term 79–80
last stand 83
second term 72–73
third term 75–79
public relations 88
  bad publicity 15
  positive 37
Puebla 10, 47
Puente 45
Puerto Plata
  exile in 87
Puerto Rico 19

Q
Querétaro 81

R
Rancho de Posadas,
  Battle of 46
revolts
  September 12, 1828 11
  September 9, 1841 11
Rio Grande 70

S
San Antonio 15, 66–67
  battles in 53, 55–56,
    61, 71
  settlements near 22,
    24, 26–27, 58
San Antonio de Bexar 6,
  31, 54, 74
San Antonio River 27,
  61
San Diego 32
San Felipe 51
San Jacinto
  defeat at 63–72
San Jacinto River 68
San Juan e Ulúa
  imprisonment in 86
Santa Anna, Antonio
  López (father) 10
  and politics 16
Santa Anna, Antonio
  (son) 42

Santa Anna, Francisca
(sister) 10
arrests 11, 46
and politics 11, 46
Santa Anna, Guadalupe
(daughter) 42, 45
Santa Anna, Manuel
(brother) 79
and the military 10
Santa Anna, Manuel
(son) 42
Santa Anna, María del
Carmen (daughter)
42
Santiesteban del Puerto
21
Santo Domingo 19
Scott, Winfield 80
Sierra Gorda region 30
slavery 40, 50
smallpox 19
Smith, John
defender of the Alamo
54
Spain
army 14, 16, 19–20,
25–27, 31, 44
colonies 11, 16, 19–28
conquistadors 11,
19–21, 23
government 12, 16,
30–32, 36–37, 39, 74
laws 25
missionaries 19–20,
25, 27
royalists 16, 28, 31,
33–37, 45
trade 15
Spanish Inquisition 16
statues 76, 78
St. Thomas
exile in 83
Sutherland, John
defender of the Alamo
54–55

T
Tamarindo 32
Tampico port 72

Taylor, Zachary 80
Tejanos 41, 51, 75
Tejas tribe 23
Tennessee regulars 8, 65
Texas 34
government 68
immigrants 51
independence 70,
77–78
independence battles
15, 48, 50, 52–70, 84
Peace Party 52
rebels in 28, 30–31, 40,
50–70, 74, 84–85
settlements 19–25, 27,
39–41, 51–52, 56–57,
67–68
territory 18, 39, 51,
70–71, 77–78
War Party 52
Texas Rangers 52
Texas War for
Independence 52–53
Texians 41, 65
battles against 9, 52, 74
Teziutlán
move to 10
Tolome 45
Tonkawa tribe 18–19
Tornel y Mendívil, José
María 37, 49, 78, 82
Tosta, Dolores (wife)
78–79, 87
Travis, William Barrett
death 65
defender of the Alamo
34, 55, 57–61, 65–67,
84
and Texas
independence 52–55
treason 86
Treaties of Córdoba 37
Treaty of Guadalupe
Hidalgo 20, 82
Treaty of Zavaleta 47

U
United States of America
44, 46, 68

army 19–20
constitution 39
government 20, 25,
39, 52, 71, 76–77,
80, 88
historians 84
military 54, 74, 76,
79–82, 84
occupation of Mexico
15
public 15
reforms 48
U.S Common Rifle 74
Utah 20

V
Veracruz 9, 11
architecture 15
capture of 80
caudillo of 40
climate 14, 30
disease in 14–15,
45–46
French blockade at
72
government 32–33, 36,
42–43, 45
home in 10, 16, 19,
28–29, 31–32, 38,
40–41, 72, 74, 79, 82,
84, 86, 88
industries in 15, 42
liberation 36–37, 88
people of 14, 76
population 14
port city of 14–15, 19,
21, 29, 72, 76, 80
raids in 15
railroad in 12
slaves in 15
tourism 15
trade 42
Veracruz University
12
Victoria, Queen of
England 77

W
weapons 74–75, 84

With Santa Anna in Texas (Peña) 84–85
Wyoming 20

X
Xalapa 28
  birthplace 9–11
  education in 12
  hacienda in 11, 40, 46, 80
  history of 11–12, 14
  imprisonment in 79
  industries in 12
  liberation 36
  political world of 11
  textile industry in 11
  trade 11, 37
Xamapa 32

Y
yellow fever 14–15, 30, 45–46

Z
Zacatecas 44

About the Author

Brenda Lange has been a writer and editor for more than 20 years. During that time, she has written for newspapers, magazines, trade publications, and a wide variety of business clientele. *Santa Anna* is her eighth book for Chelsea House. She also has revised two other titles. Lange is a member of the American Society of Journalists and Authors (ASJA) and the Society of Professional Journalists (SPJ) and lives and works in Doylestown, Pennsylvania. www.brendalange.com